THE TEN PILLARS
of Owning and Operating
A SUCCESSFUL BUSINESS

by Samantha Zayas

Edited by Lil Barcaski and Kristen Winiarski

PUBLISHED BY: GWN Publishing

www.GWNPublishing.com

COVER DESIGN: Kristina Conatser

ISBN: 978-1-959608-79-0

DEDICATION

To all business owners and entrepreneurs who tirelessly pursue their dreams and ambitions, and to my family and friends whose unwavering support has been the cornerstone of my journey.

CONTENTS

A LETTER FROM THE AUTHOR

Dear Readers,

I am incredibly excited and honored to present to you my book, *The Ten Pillars of Owning and Operating a Successful Business*. As I sit down to write this letter, I am overcome with gratitude for the opportunity to share my experiences, insights, and hard-earned wisdom with all of you.

This book is the culmination of a lifelong journey filled with struggles, setbacks, and triumphs. From my earliest memories, I was raised in a dysfunctional home, where physical and mental violence were all too common. As a foster child, I faced the challenges of navigating a system that often fell short of meeting my needs. My mother battled mental health issues, and my father grappled with addiction. We lived below the poverty line, relying on public assistance just to survive.

Becoming a single teenage mother added an additional layer of complexity to my journey. The responsibilities and pressures of parenthood were overwhelming at times, but they also fueled a deep desire within me to create a better life for myself and my children. I was determined to break the cycle of poverty, rise above my circumstances, and build a future filled with success and abundance.

But let me be honest with you—the path to success was far from easy. It was a road paved with failures, disappointments, and moments of self-doubt. I experienced setbacks that made me question my abilities and my worth. And yet, through it all, I never lost sight of my vision for a better life.

Success is neither defined by your ethnicity nor country of origin. Success is for anyone and everyone who desires change. We all have the power to change the trajectory of our life.

The ten pillars outlined in this book are the result of years of personal growth, extensive research, and learning from both my own experiences and the experiences of successful entrepreneurs around the world. These pillars are the guiding principles that have helped me navigate the often treacherous waters of owning and operating a business.

In *The Ten Pillars of Owning and Operating a Successful Business*, you will find a comprehensive framework that covers every aspect of entrepreneurship. From identifying your target market and crafting a compelling vision to building a strong team and implementing effective marketing strategies, each pillar is designed to provide you with the knowledge and tools you need to succeed.

But let me be clear—this book is not a magic formula for instant success. It is not a shortcut or a guarantee of overnight riches. Owning and operating a successful business is a journey that requires dedication, perseverance, and a willingness to learn from both successes and failures.

I encourage you to approach this book with an open mind and a willingness to implement the principles and strategies outlined within its pages. Adapt them to your unique circumstances, test them, and refine them as you go.

Remember, the path to success is not a straight line, but a winding road filled with twists and turns. Embrace the challenges, celebrate the victories, and never lose sight of your ultimate goals.

I want to express my deepest gratitude for joining me on this journey. It is my sincerest hope that *The Ten Pillars of Owning and Operating a Successful Business* will serve as a source of inspiration, guidance, and motivation as you embark on your own entrepreneurial endeavors. May these pillars become the foundation upon which you construct a thriving and fulfilling business that not only brings you financial success but also enables you to make a positive impact in the world.

Thank you for your trust and support. I am honored to be a part of your journey toward success.

Warmest regards,

Samantha Zayas

INTRODUCTION

I've had my fair share of struggles, but I firmly believe that it's up to me to change the course of my life. You might be wondering who I am. Well, let me tell you about my journey and the hardships I've faced since I was a young child.

Success is within reach for anyone who is willing to put in the hard work and change their trajectory. It doesn't matter where you come from or what your ethnic background is. I firmly believe that. I've seen it in my own life.

I have two incredible children, and they have always been my motivation to strive for more. I knew I had to break the cycle of poverty and break free from the grips of my past. It's been a journey of self-discovery, growth, and determination.

Failure has been a constant companion on this journey, but I've learned to embrace it. Each setback has taught me valuable lessons and given me the strength to persevere. It hasn't been easy, but I've come to realize that my life is what I make of it.

I want to emphasize that success is possible for anyone who is willing to work hard and make the necessary changes. It may not be a smooth road, and there will be obstacles along the way, but with determination and a positive mindset, we can overcome them.

I've also learned the importance of seeking support. Surrounding myself with positive influences and finding mentors and role models who have overcome similar challenges has made a significant difference. Building a strong support network has been crucial to my progress.

So, if you're going through tough times, remember that you have the power to shape your own future. Don't underestimate your own strength and resilience. Keep pushing forward, stay focused on your goals, and never lose sight of the fact that you have the ability to create the life you desire.

WHO THIS BOOK IS FOR

This book is for individuals who are eager to venture into the world of business or those who have already started their own businesses, but have hit a plateau and are seeking ways to achieve greater success. If you are someone who wants to learn how to pivot, change, learn, and grow your business, then this book is for you. I wrote this book based on my personal experiences of starting multiple businesses and becoming a multi-millionaire in my early thirties. My goal is to provide you with the foundation and step-by-step guidance you need to become a successful business owner.

If you are new to the business world, you may have a business idea in mind but lack the knowledge and actionable steps to bring that idea to life. *Ten Pillars* is designed to walk you through the process of starting a business venture and offer valuable insights and strategies to set you on the right path.

Even if you are already running a business, you may find yourself feeling stuck and struggling to achieve the growth you desire. This book aims to address those challenges head-on and provide you with practical advice on how to overcome obstacles, make necessary changes, and propel your business forward.

As someone who loves attending conferences and trainings, and implementing what I learned, I understand the frustration of attending conferences or seminars where you gather a multitude of ideas but lack the specific steps to put them into action. In this book, I provide you with the actual steps and guidance you need to turn your ideas and concepts into tangible results.

Whether you are a newcomer to the business world or an existing business owner seeking accelerated growth, this book is tailored to equip you with the knowledge, strategies, and actionable steps required to achieve your goals as a successful business owner. It is my hope that you will find inspiration, practical insights, and the motivation to take your business to new heights.

It's true that there are numerous business books out there that provide valuable information and inspiration. However, many of them fail to bridge the gap between lofty ideas and practical implementation. This disconnect often leaves readers wondering how to translate those ideas into actionable steps.

In this book, I aim to address this issue by offering concrete tools, actionable steps, and practical advice that you can implement in your own entrepreneurial journey. I want this book to be more than just a one-time read for you. I want it to serve as a valuable resource that you can refer back to as you navigate different stages of your business growth.

By providing you with actual tools and actionable items, my intention is to ensure that you have a clear path to follow in order to make your ideas a reality. I want you to feel equipped and empowered to take action and see tangible results.

Let's begin by examining the conventional ways in which most people get started in business. By understanding the common pitfalls and challenges entrepreneurs face at the outset, we can lay a strong foundation for your journey. Throughout the book, I will guide you step-by-step, sharing insights, strategies, and practical advice to help you overcome obstacles and achieve the success you desire.

WHEN PEOPLE GET AN INSPIRATION

Many people experience moments of inspiration and excitement that lead them to consider starting a business. However, without proper planning and research, they can quickly find themselves stuck and facing various challenges.

In this book, I want to emphasize the importance of asking critical questions and conducting thorough research before diving headfirst into starting a business. Rushing into entrepreneurship without proper preparation can lead to wasted time, money, and effort.

BY TAKING THE TIME TO ASK YOURSELF IMPORTANT QUESTIONS AND CONDUCT RESEARCH, YOU CAN GAIN A CLEARER UNDERSTANDING OF YOUR BUSINESS IDEA AND ITS POTENTIAL VIABILITY. SOME QUESTIONS YOU MAY CONSIDER INCLUDE:

- What problem does my business solve?
- Who are my target customers or clients?
- Is there a market demand for my product or service?
- Who are my competitors, and how can I differentiate myself?
- What resources and skills do I need to succeed in this industry?
- What is my unique value proposition?
- How will I reach and attract customers or clients?
- What are the potential risks and challenges I may encounter?

By thoroughly researching and answering these questions, you can make informed decisions and develop a solid foundation for your business. This will help you avoid common pitfalls and increase your chances of long-term success.

You will find a page at the end of each chapter where you can add your own thoughts and reflections on what you learned in the chapter. Consider the action items and write down how they might be used to assist you in your business.

In this book, I will guide you through the process of asking the right questions and conducting the necessary research.

By doing so, you will gain the knowledge and insights needed to make informed decisions and set yourself up for success in your entrepreneurial journey.

After countless nights of research, I was driven to fill this gap for other parents who were facing similar situations. That's when I decided to take matters into my own hands.

Education has always been a top priority for me and my family. I firmly believe that children should have access to early literacy and learning opportunities. However, in our community, there was a lack of funding and resources for early education. This resulted in many children struggling with reading and writing skills by the time they reached middle school. I didn't want my children or any other child to experience that setback.

To fulfill this need, I took the leap and opened my own school. By doing so, I aimed to provide a safe and nurturing environment where children could thrive academically while their parents focused on their jobs. I wanted to offer not just childcare, but a comprehensive educational experience.

Starting my own school required careful planning and research. I sought out qualified educators who shared my passion for education and hired them to be part of my team. Together, we developed a curriculum that emphasized early literacy, numeracy, and holistic child development. We created engaging learning environments and invested in educational resources to support children's growth.

Securing funding for my venture was challenging since there were no available resources in our area. However, I explored various options, including personal savings and loans, to finance the initial setup costs. I also reached out to local businesses and community organizations, explaining the importance of early education and seeking their support through sponsorships or partnerships.

Marketing played a vital role in spreading the word about my school. I utilized both traditional methods, like distributing flyers and brochures, and modern strategies, such as establishing an online presence through a website and social media platforms. Through these efforts, I aimed to connect with parents who shared the same concerns and values when it came to their children's education.

As my school grew, I remained committed to continuous improvement. I regularly evaluated our educational programs, sought feedback from parents, and made adjustments to meet the evolving needs of the children in our care. It was essential for me to maintain open lines of communication with parents, fostering a collaborative relationship to support their children's educational journey.

By starting my own school, I not only addressed my personal need as a working parent but also filled a significant gap in our community. I was able to provide children with a nurturing environment where they could develop essential skills and a love for learning from an early age. Witnessing their progress and knowing that I was making a positive impact on their lives and futures was incredibly rewarding.

I was also able to address two pressing needs simultaneously. First, I no longer had to worry about leaving my children with strangers who couldn't provide them with a quality education. Second, I had the opportunity to earn a living by meeting the needs of other families in a similar situation while making a difference in the community and the lives of children.

Before diving into this venture, I conducted thorough research to gather relevant information. I examined the local community to understand the number of children in different age groups and the average income of families in the area who might require the services of my school. Additionally, I assessed the existing competition to identify what set me apart and how I could be the best resource for families like my own.

To gain further guidance and insights, I reached out to the local Small Business Development Center (SBDC). They provided valuable advice on start-up costs and helped me create a comprehensive plan to follow. We conducted a profits and loss (P&L) analysis, working backward to determine the financial aspects of the business. I calculated how much revenue I needed to generate by considering factors such as rent, desired profit margin, and the number of students required to achieve profitability.

This detailed analysis allowed me to set appropriate pricing for my services and ensured I had a clear understanding of the financial feasibility of my business. It also helped me establish realistic goals and timelines for breaking even and achieving profitability.

In addition to the financial aspects, I also focused on developing a unique value proposition that would differentiate my school from the competition. I carefully considered what I could do differently to stand out as the preferred choice for families seeking quality education and care. This involved creating a well-rounded curriculum, hiring qualified and passionate staff, providing a nurturing environment, and offering additional value-added services that catered to the specific needs of the families I aimed to serve.

By conducting thorough research, seeking guidance, and strategically planning the financial and competitive aspects of my school, I laid a solid foundation for success. This allowed me to confidently move forward, knowing I had a clear vision and a well-defined strategy to fulfill the needs of families in my community while creating a sustainable and profitable business.

You know what? Opening a business is not as simple as it seems. I often see people making this mistake. They think just because they are good at cooking, they should open a restaurant. Or because they have a lot of friends, they believe they could run a successful bar. But let me tell you, that's more of a hobby than a real business. There's so much more to consider.

Let's take the example of rising food costs. What would you do if the prices of the ingredients you need skyrocketed? You can't just ignore it and hope for the best. You need to make some adjustments. Maybe you have to change your prices or make the portions smaller to maintain your profitability. And don't forget to check what the restaurant up the block is charging for similar menus. You have to stay competitive if you want to survive.

And then there are those who try to open clothing stores. Seriously, have they not heard of Amazon? With the convenience of online shopping, where things are delivered right to your doorstep and returns are a breeze, why would people bother going to a physical store? It's just not practical anymore, or if you do decide to do this, you must understand what will make your business different and unique to keep up with the changing market.

It baffles me when people say they want to be their own boss, become entrepreneurs, but they fail to think through all the details. It's great to want to become your own boss and an entrepreneur. That's why I'm here to break it down for you. We need to go through each and every element of running a business and explain what it really entails. And, of course, I'll provide you with some action items and tools to help you navigate through it all.

First and foremost, you need to know your market. Who are your customers? What do they want? Then, we can dive into the nitty-gritty of business planning, marketing and sales strategies, operations and logistics, customer experience and service, and financial management. It's not an easy journey, but with careful consideration and the right tools, you can increase your chances of success.

So, before you jump into starting your own business, make sure you've thought it through. Take the time to understand your market, analyze the competition, and assess the feasibility of your venture. Being an entrepreneur and business owner requires attention to detail and continuous learning. Stay informed about industry trends and embrace new technologies. Only then can you truly thrive in the business world.

We are going to break this down for you into sections with explanations of what each element of business entails. And in each section, you will have action items and tools. There are so many moving parts to consider before you get into business and even after you are in business for some time.

HOW TO USE THIS BOOK MOST EFFECTIVELY

THROUGHOUT THIS BOOK, AT THE END OF EACH CHAPTER, THERE WILL BE ACTION ITEMS FOR YOU TO MAKE USE OF RIGHT AWAY AND A LINED PAGE TO WRITE NOTES OR REFLECTIONS. BY TAKING IMMEDIATE ACTION ON THESE ADDITIONAL ITEMS, YOUR BUSINESS CAN FURTHER BENEFIT AND TRANSFORM IN VARIOUS WAYS:

- Improved strategic alignment and goal attainment.
- Enhanced leadership effectiveness and team productivity.
- Increased brand recognition and market share.
- Streamlined processes and reduced operational costs.
- Better financial planning and investment decisions.
- Deeper customer relationships and loyalty.
- Cultivated culture of innovation and adaptability.
- Attraction and retention of top talent.
- Enhanced reputation as an ethical business.

▶ Effective risk mitigation and business continuity.

Remember, these suggestions are not exhaustive, and the specific actions you choose will depend on your business's unique needs and goals. Regularly reassess your business's progress and make adjustments as necessary to ensure continued success.

1

VISION AND STRATEGY: DRIVING ORGANIZATIONAL SUCCESS

YOUR VISION IS KEY!

In this chapter, I will discuss the importance of having a clear vision and strategy to drive organizational success.

I started my business in childcare with a vision to help parents like myself and create a long-term solution for high-quality education and care in my community. I had a passion for childcare and children, and I wanted to make a positive change for both my own children and the people around me.

To begin, it is crucial to identify a problem that no one else is solving. This problem will be the foundation of your vision. Ask yourself how you can address this problem and if you have the ability to solve it.

I created a roadmap outlining every step necessary to succeed in my vision. It wasn't enough for me to simply declare that I wanted to be a coach, a restaurateur, or a childcare center owner. I started by asking myself what it would take to be successful. How many students, clients, or customers would I need to sustain my business?

In my case, I determined that I needed 20 students to cover all my expenses, including rent, staff salaries, utilities, and other costs. I also realized I wanted to be an active owner, involved in every aspect of my business. While some may dream of being absent owners, I recognized that, especially at the beginning, it was important for me to be hands-on.

To accurately gauge what I needed to cover costs, I carefully examined every aspect of doing business and calculated the associated expenses. This allowed me to have a realistic understanding of the financial requirements and set achievable goals.

By having a clear grasp of the financial aspects and costs, I could determine the number of customers, clients, or students required to sustain my business. This knowledge became the foundation of my strategic decisions and ensured that my roadmap was grounded in reality.

Having a detailed understanding of the financial requirements and setting realistic goals enabled me to stay focused and make informed decisions as I worked toward the success of my vision.

Let's look at how knowledge of financial needs and attainable goals might work for other ventures.

If you are deciding to go into coaching, you will need to know the number of clients you need to make a living. This depends on several factors, such as your pricing structure, the time and energy you can dedicate to each client, and your desired income level. To determine the number of clients needed, you would first calculate your monthly expenses, including personal and business costs. Then, factor in a reasonable profit margin and estimate the revenue you would generate from each client.

For group coaching, determine the group size and set a price per participant that would cover your costs and provide a profit. For one-on-one coaching, it would be wise to set a higher price to account for the personalized attention and resources provided to each client.

If you are producing a product, such as organic soap, you would need to consider the production costs, including raw materials, manufacturing equipment, and facility expenses. To determine how many bars of soap you would need to sell to cover the facility costs, divide the monthly facility expenses by the profit margin per bar of soap. This calculation will give you the minimum number of sales required to cover the facility expenses.

If your business grows, you might consider hiring employees to assist with production or other tasks. The cost of employing staff would depend on factors such as wages, benefits, and any additional expenses associated with having employees. You would need to factor these costs into your pricing strategy and sales projections.

To ensure the sustainability of your business, you would need to consider customer retention and repeat business. For products like soap, you would analyze the average usage rate and the purchasing frequency of customers. This information would help you estimate the number of customers needed to maintain a steady stream of revenue.

Understanding the financial aspects of your business, including the number of customers needed, the revenue per customer, and the potential for repeat business, is crucial for long-term success. It allows you to set realistic goals, develop appropriate pricing strategies, and make informed decisions to ensure profitability and growth.

In order to enhance our services and stand out from the competition, it's crucial to offer unique and innovative solutions that address customer needs. Take laundromats, for example. Nowadays, many laundromats provide full-service options such as pick-up, wash, fold, and delivery. By incorporating such comprehensive services, we can take customer experience to a whole new level.

Another aspect to consider is the importance of service in your vision. Let's consider the example of hiring a dog-sitter. Instead of simply offering pet-sitting services, go the extra mile by providing reliable and trustworthy dog sitters who visit clients' homes to take care of their pets. By prioritizing exceptional service, you can build trust and loyalty among your customers.

When developing your vision, it's essential to incorporate these elements into your value proposition. Your value proposition are the statements that clearly define what you offer and the value of your goods and services. Your vision should be prominently displayed across various platforms, including your website, marketing materials, and social media channels. By consistently communicating your vision, you can create a strong foundation for your brand and ensure that your customers understand the unique value you offer.

Drawing from my own experience, I started by offering tours to families, where we would explain our vision and purpose. It was crucial for all of our teachers to believe in and embody this vision, so that when the children went home, they would share their positive experiences and learnings. Our goal was to ensure that children returned home happy and well-cared for, leaving no doubt in the parents' minds about the quality of our services.

VISION AND STRATEGY

Start by developing a clear and compelling vision for your business. This vision should outline your long-term aspirations and provide a sense of purpose and direction. Once you have a vision in place, create a strategic plan that breaks down your goals into actionable steps. This plan will serve as a roadmap to guide your business toward success. A clear vision provides the guiding light for a successful business. This section explores the importance of defining a compelling vision and developing a strategic plan to achieve it. It delves into elements such as mission statements, goal setting, SWOT analysis (Strengths, Weaknesses, Opportunities, and Threats as compared to other business or projects), and long-term planning.

In the dynamic and competitive landscape of today's business world, organizations require a clear vision and a well-defined strategy to navigate uncertainty, seize opportunities, and achieve sustainable success. Vision and strategy are fundamental pillars that guide decision-making, shape organizational culture, and align actions toward a common purpose. This chapter aims to explore the significance of vision and strategy, their interdependence, and their role in driving organizational success.

DEFINING VISION

A vision is a compelling and aspirational statement that outlines the desired future state of an organization. It serves as a guiding light, inspiring and motivating stakeholders by painting a vivid picture of what the organization aims to achieve. A well-crafted vision statement provides clarity, direction, and a sense of purpose to employees, customers, and partners.

THE IMPORTANCE OF VISION

A compelling vision is crucial for several reasons. Firstly, it creates a shared understanding of the organization's long-term goals, fostering unity and alignment among stakeholders. It helps employees identify with the organization's purpose and values, enhancing engagement and commitment. Additionally, a vision provides a framework for decision-making, ensuring that actions are consistent with the desired future state. Furthermore, a well-communicated vision attracts and retains talent since individuals are drawn to organizations with a clear sense of direction and purpose.

THE ESSENCE OF STRATEGY

While a vision sets the destination, strategy outlines the roadmap to reach that destination. Strategy involves a series of deliberate choices and actions that allocate resources, define competitive advantages, and position the organization for success. It involves analyzing the external environment, identifying opportunities and threats, and leveraging internal capabilities to achieve strategic objectives.

THE INTERPLAY BETWEEN VISION AND STRATEGY

Vision and strategy are inseparable and interdependent. A vision provides the overarching purpose and direction, while strategy defines the specific actions required to achieve the vision. The vision acts as a guiding principle, ensuring that the strategy remains focused on the ultimate objective. Conversely, a well-crafted strategy supports the realization of the vision by breaking it down into actionable steps and milestones. Both vision and strategy are iterative and adaptive, requiring periodic review and refinement to address changing market dynamics.

ALIGNING VISION AND STRATEGY WITH ORGANIZATIONAL CULTURE

To be effective, a vision and strategy must be aligned with the organization's culture. Culture embodies the shared values, beliefs, and behaviors that shape how work is done.

When the vision and strategy are congruent with the culture, they are more likely to be embraced and executed effectively. Leaders play a critical role in fostering a culture that supports the vision and strategy, promoting collaboration, innovation, and continuous improvement.

DRIVING ORGANIZATIONAL SUCCESS

An organization with a clear vision and a well-defined strategy is better equipped to achieve success. Vision and strategy provide a framework for decision-making, enabling organizations to prioritize resources, invest in the right initiatives, and adapt to changing circumstances. They create a sense of direction and purpose, motivating employees and aligning their efforts toward common goals. Moreover, vision and strategy enhance organizational resilience, as they provide a roadmap to overcome challenges and seize opportunities.

In conclusion, vision and strategy are indispensable elements that drive organizational success. A compelling vision inspires and guides stakeholders, while a well-crafted strategy outlines the actions required to achieve the vision. Both vision and strategy must be aligned with the organization's culture to maximize their impact. Together, they provide a roadmap for navigating uncertainty and sustainable growth in a competitive business landscape. By setting a clear direction, engaging employees, and making informed decisions, organizations can effectively allocate resources, adapt to change, and seize opportunities. Vision and strategy act as beacons, guiding organizations toward their desired future state and enabling them to thrive in an ever-evolving marketplace.

ACTIONABLE ITEMS
TO PUT INTO PLACE

☒ Develop a mission statement that clearly defines the purpose and values of your business.

☒ Create a visual representation of your vision and display it prominently in your workplace.

☒ Break down your strategic plan into quarterly or monthly objectives to track progress and make adjustments as needed.

☒ Conduct a vision and goal-setting workshop with your team to ensure everyone is aligned with the company's direction.

☒ Create visual representations of your vision and goals, such as vision boards or mission statements, and display them prominently in your workspace.

REFLECTIONS

2

MARKET RESEARCH AND CUSTOMER FOCUS

Research is key before you get into business. There are many things to consider before you get started.

If you are opening a brick-and-mortar business, you must research the physical area where you are looking to go into business. Demographics are key.

Is the business you want to start needed in the location you're considering? The old adage location, location, location is real. If you choose the wrong location, it could set you up for failure. Whether it's a childcare center, a restaurant, a medical facility or any customer-focused business, you need to do the homework to know what the demographics are in the surrounding area, and research the location you are considering for traffic patterns, foot traffic, and, of course, competition. What other businesses are like yours, how close are they, what do they offer that you do, and what about you is different?

Am I in an area where people will find me? Who lives and works there? Are they mostly families or singles? What is the mean average age range and average household income? All those things matter to any business. You just need to know who your ideal clients and avatar will be, and if they will be likely to come to you where you are planning to set up shop.

If you are a global business with no geolocation, you still need to do your demographics. Your clients will be online, but you need to know where they hang out. Which social media platforms have the target audience you're seeking? People who spend more time on Facebook or Pinterest are different from the LinkedIn crowd or the TikTok crew. There are tons of groups; women's groups, writers, parents, military, business coaches and everything possible. You need to know what groups to join and what the rules of engagement are to be able to market to the members. Facebook ads will let you target age, location, sex, income, and other things. If you know who you are looking for, ads can be worth spending money on. Every business is unique and has its own concept.

Imagine you have a clothing line exclusively designed for older women. It's important to understand that your marketing efforts should be directed toward your target audience. In this case, it's unlikely that men or parents of young children would be the primary customers. To effectively reach the right customers, you need to identify who can afford your high-end clothing. Conducting thorough research becomes essential to gain a clear understanding of your target market.

Start by researching and determining the demographic that aligns with your clothing line. Consider factors such as age, lifestyle, occupation, and income level. This will help you create a detailed profile of your ideal customer.

By doing so, you can refine your marketing strategies and tailor them specifically to this segment.

Understanding the purchasing power of your target audience is crucial, especially if your clothing line is high-end. Conduct market research to identify the income levels, spending habits, and financial capacities of your potential customers. This information will help you position your brand and determine appropriate pricing strategies.

Being targeted and specific in your marketing efforts requires a deep understanding of your customers' preferences and needs. Research their fashion preferences, style choices, and overall expectations of clothing. This knowledge will enable you to curate a collection that resonates with their tastes and meets their requirements.

Furthermore, conducting market research allows you to identify any gaps in the market that your clothing line can fill. Analyze the competition and understand their target market, pricing strategies, and unique selling points. This analysis will help you differentiate your brand and create a compelling value proposition.

Remember, effective marketing relies on being precise and focused. By conducting thorough research, you can gain insights into your target market's demographics, purchasing power, preferences, and unmet needs. This knowledge will guide your marketing strategies and ensure that your clothing line for older women reaches the right audience, driving success for your business.

In establishing my childcare centers, I prioritized understanding the demographics and income levels of my target market. Through surveys and direct mail campaigns, I targeted families with children who had the financial means to afford tuition. Analyzing the average median income of the area helped me determine appropriate tuition costs and select strategic locations. This research-driven approach proved instrumental in the success of my childcare businesses.

You also need to know your differentiator. For me, I found that offering a strong education alongside childcare services was my key differentiator. The schools I established were located in more rural areas, where there was little to no competition. This made it convenient and easy for parents to drop off and pick up their children, as the schools were not out of their way. Even though it may seem like a small detail, I specifically chose locations with easy-to-pull-into intersections, so parents didn't have to turn around on busy roads or face difficulties while picking up their children. They could simply line up and quickly retrieve their children without any hassle. I firmly believe that convenience is something people truly value and appreciate.

Another important factor to consider is visibility. When it comes to physical locations, it's crucial that people can easily see your business from the road. Having clear and readable signage that is large enough is essential. On the other hand, if you run an online business, it's essential to appear on the first page of Google search results. Being buried on page ten won't do you any good. It's like having a bad location. Additionally, leveraging social media platforms is crucial for both online and physical businesses to enhance their visibility. Being easily discoverable on people's mobile phones is a must.

Restaurants, in particular, heavily rely on high visibility. They need to keep a close eye on the competition and find ways to stand out. Offering a unique and exceptional experience becomes a critical part of their marketing strategy. Moreover, quality is of utmost importance. If you can't offer a one-of-a-kind experience, then it becomes crucial to be better than your competitors in terms of quality.

My childcare centers are located in areas where there are no corporate private schools nearby. In my region, people have to travel approximately seven to ten miles to access childcare services. To gauge the potential interest in my services, I conducted an online survey targeted at specific zip codes. I actively engaged with family groups on social media to gather valuable insights. I invested time and effort into conducting thorough research.

When it comes to businesses like mechanics, tire shops, and quick oil change places, it's not uncommon to see an excessive concentration of such establishments in one area. However, if you're considering opening a franchise or a similar shop in the same vicinity, it might be worth considering doing something different instead. Setting yourself apart from the competition can be a wise strategy.

Ultimately, the key takeaway is that conducting extensive research before opening a business can save you a lot of headaches and heartaches down the line. By investing more time upfront in understanding the market, customer needs, and potential competition, you can make informed decisions and increase your chances of success.

Market research and customer focus are integral components of a successful business strategy. Understanding the market landscape, identifying customer needs, and delivering value-driven solutions are essential for gaining a competitive edge and achieving sustainable growth. This chapter explores the importance of market research, the significance of customer focus, and the ways in which organizations can effectively leverage these concepts to drive business success.

Understanding your target market is essential for developing products and services that meet customer needs. Conduct thorough market research analysis to gather insights about your customers, their preferences, and staying abreast of overall market trends. Utilize this information to create customer personas, identify key market segments, and tailor your offerings to provide unique value and a superior customer experience.

Market research and customer focus are critical elements for organizations seeking to thrive in a competitive business environment. By conducting comprehensive market research and understanding customer preferences, businesses can build strong customer relationships, and drive sustainable growth. Integrating market research and customer focus allows organizations to make informed decisions, tailor their offerings to meet customer needs, and create exceptional customer experiences. By continuously monitoring the market, analyzing customer feedback, and adapting strategies accordingly, organizations can stay ahead of the competition and build long-term success.

THE IMPORTANCE OF MARKET RESEARCH

Market research involves the systematic collection and analysis of data to gain insights into the market, industry trends, customer behavior, and competitors. It provides organizations with valuable information to make informed decisions and develop effective strategies.

KEY REASONS FOR CONDUCTING MARKET RESEARCH INCLUDE:

a. Understanding customer preferences, needs, and buying behavior.
b. Identifying market opportunities, gaps, and emerging trends.
c. Assessing the competitive landscape and positioning.
d. Evaluating the effectiveness of marketing campaigns and initiatives.
e. Mitigating risks and making data-driven decisions.

MARKET RESEARCH METHODS

THERE ARE VARIOUS METHODS FOR CONDUCTING MARKET RESEARCH, INCLUDING:

a. Surveys and questionnaires to gather quantitative and qualitative data.

b. Interviews and focus groups to obtain in-depth insights from target customers.

c. Data analysis of existing customer databases, sales figures, and online metrics.

d. Competitor analysis to understand their strategies, strengths, and weaknesses.

e. Observational research to study customer behavior in real-life settings.

f. Trend analysis and forecasting to anticipate future market developments.

CUSTOMER FOCUS

Customer focus is centered on understanding and meeting the needs and expectations of customers. It involves building strong relationships, delivering exceptional experiences, and continuously improving products or services.

KEY ASPECTS OF CUSTOMER FOCUS INCLUDE:

a. Market segmentation to identify specific customer groups and their unique requirements.

b. Customer journey mapping to understand the customer's interactions and touchpoints.

c. Personalization and customization to tailor offerings to individual customer preferences.

d. Building trust and loyalty through excellent customer service and support.

e. Obtaining customer feedback and actively listening to their opinions and suggestions.

BENEFITS OF CUSTOMER FOCUS

ORGANIZATIONS THAT PRIORITIZE CUSTOMER FOCUS CAN REAP SEVERAL BENEFITS, SUCH AS:

a. Increased customer satisfaction and loyalty, leading to repeat business and referrals.
b. Improved brand reputation and positive word-of-mouth recommendations.
c. Enhanced ability to anticipate and adapt to changing customer needs and preferences.
d. Higher customer retention rates and lower customer acquisition costs.
e. Greater competitive advantage by offering unique value propositions.

INTEGRATING MARKET RESEARCH AND CUSTOMER FOCUS

TO EFFECTIVELY LEVERAGE MARKET RESEARCH AND CUSTOMER FOCUS, ORGANIZATIONS SHOULD:

a. Align market research objectives with strategic business goals.
b. Use market research findings to identify customer segments and target markets.

c. Develop customer-centric strategies based on market insights and customer needs.

d. Continuously monitor and analyze market trends, competitor activities, and customer feedback.

e. Regularly update and refine products, services, and marketing approaches based on customer insights.

f. Foster a culture of customer-centricity throughout the organization.

In conclusion, market research and customer focus are vital for organizations aiming to understand their target markets, identify customer needs, and deliver value. By conducting thorough market research, organizations can gather valuable insights and make data-driven decisions. Additionally, by prioritizing customer focus, organizations can build strong customer relationships, enhance customer satisfaction and loyalty, and gain a competitive advantage. Integrating market research and customer focus into business strategies allows organizations to anticipate market trends, stay relevant, and drive growth in today's dynamic business landscape.

ACTIONABLE ITEMS
TO PUT INTO PLACE

- ☒ Conduct surveys, interviews, and focus groups regularly to gather ongoing customer insights.

- ☒ Utilize data analytics tools to analyze customer behavior, preferences, and purchasing patterns.

- ☒ Stay updated on industry trends through market research reports, industry publications, and attending relevant conferences or events.

- ☒ Implement regular one-on-one meetings with your team members to provide individual guidance, support, and feedback.

- ☒ Invest in leadership development programs or external coaching to enhance your own leadership skills.

REFLECTIONS

3

QUALITY PRODUCTS OR SERVICES

As I mentioned in the previous chapter, quality can make a significant difference in business. Even when offering the same product or service as competitors, you can outshine them by delivering better quality. For instance, using fresher and superior ingredients in food preparation can result in tastier dishes, attracting more customers. The same applies to products requiring craftsmanship, such as clothing, skincare items, soaps, and personal hygiene products. It's important to ensure the best possible quality within your chosen price range.

In today's market, creating innovative products can also drive business success. While not everyone can come up with the next big thing, introducing new products, apps, or innovations can set you apart. It's an opportunity to capture the attention of customers and gain a competitive edge.

If you're in the service industry, expanding your offerings with additional services is a powerful strategy for long-term business growth. Acquiring new clients can be challenging, but once you earn their trust and they become satisfied with your services, they are more likely to engage with you for other services you provide.

For example, in the childcare industry, offering before- and after-school programs can be a valuable addition to your existing services. Similarly, laundromats have started offering convenient services such as pick-up, wash and fold, and delivery, which have become particularly popular during the Covid-19 pandemic and have continued to be in demand.

To identify additional services that can bring more convenience and value to your clients, be open to adaptation and improvement. Listen to customer feedback and understand their needs and pain points. This will help you tailor your offerings and enhance customer service. Embracing new innovations and technology can also contribute to customer satisfaction and loyalty.

By consistently providing excellent customer service, adding new services, and staying innovative, you can create a positive customer experience that encourages referrals and repeat business. This approach fosters customer loyalty and enables you to build a strong client base that continuously supports your business.

ACTIONABLE ITEMS
TO PUT INTO PLACE

☒ Establish a quality assurance program that includes rigorous testing, inspections, and customer feedback loops.

☒ Conduct regular product/service reviews to identify areas for improvement and innovation.

☒ Implement a continuous improvement process to refine your offerings based on customer feedback and changing market demands.

☒ Conduct market research to gain a deeper understanding of your target audience's needs and preferences.

☒ Develop a content marketing strategy and create valuable, informative content that resonates with your target audience.

REFLECTIONS

4

EFFECTIVE LEADERSHIP AND MANAGEMENT

As the owner of a business, I understand the vital role that strong leadership plays in achieving success. I believe that my active involvement and guidance are essential for effectively managing my team. By providing strong leadership, I can inspire and motivate both my staff and shareholders.

I consider myself a visionary, often generating big ideas that drive the direction of our company. I recognize that my managers and directors are the backbone of our organization. They are responsible for implementing my vision and ensuring that it permeates throughout the company. To prepare them for unexpected challenges, I invest time in training them to navigate storms that may arise. The COVID-19 pandemic serves as a prime example of such a challenge.

During the pandemic, we faced daily uncertainties and had to make rapid changes. Nevertheless, I am proud to say that my team leaders remained confident and well-versed in our ever-evolving policies and procedures. This allowed us to adapt swiftly and effectively during this difficult time.

In any company or business, it's crucial that everyone shares the same mission, vision, and drive for growth and success. From the owner to the entire staff, we all need to be on the same page. Imagine it like rowing a boat—if we're all rowing in different directions without a common goal, we won't make any progress. We'll just end up going in circles like a hamster on a wheel.

As the owner, it's our responsibility to teach our team leaders about our vision and mission. They, in turn, pass it on to the rest of the staff. This ensures that our business runs smoothly, like a well-oiled machine. Without a strong leader, confusion and mistrust can creep in. All it takes is one person who doesn't see or believe in the vision or becomes disgruntled to bring the whole business down. That's why managers need to have a strong backbone and be willing to address and change those dynamics or remove the person causing problems. It's important to take action and fix things immediately.

By fostering a culture of unity, trust, and quick resolution of issues, we can ensure that everyone is rowing in the same direction. This promotes efficiency, productivity, and ultimately leads to the growth and success of our business.

It is important to invest in leadership development programs for yourself and key members of your management team. Foster open and transparent communication channels to ensure alignment with your team. Always lead by example, demonstrating the values and behaviors you expect from your employees. Encourage cross-functional collaboration and provide opportunities for employees to work on diverse projects.

In today's business landscape, open and transparent communication is absolutely essential. We often struggle with effective communication due to our heavy reliance on texts and emails, which make it hard to have difficult conversations. Face-to-face talks seem to be a rarity these days. As a leader, it's crucial to address this challenge and empower our team members to enhance their communication skills. This way, we can avoid constantly dealing with crises and focus on more important tasks.

One way to tackle this issue is by nurturing strong leaders within our organization. When we try to do everything ourselves, we end up being ineffective at everything. By developing and empowering our team leaders, we can distribute the workload and create a more balanced and efficient work environment. Strong leaders are adept at communicating with their teams, addressing challenges directly, and handling tough conversations.

To build strong leaders, we need to provide them with the necessary skills and resources to excel in their roles. This includes helping them improve their communication abilities, sharpen their decision-making skills, and foster their problem-solving capabilities. Additionally, as leaders, we should inspire and motivate our team members, nurturing a positive work culture that encourages collaboration and innovation.

By emphasizing effective communication and cultivating strong leadership, we establish a foundation for success in our business. A culture that values integrity, accountability, and open dialogue will contribute to the growth and prosperity of our organization.

ACTIONABLE ITEMS
TO PUT INTO PLACE

- ☒ Identify key performance indicators (KPI) for each department and establish regular monitoring and reporting mechanisms.

- ☒ Implement project management, tools, or software to streamline project, workflow, and improvement collaboration.

- ☒ Develop a comprehensive onboarding process to ensure new employees quickly integrate into your company culture.

- ☒ Create standard operating procedures (SOP's) which are step-by-step, clear policies and procedures. To ensure easier and better workflow.

- ☒ Establish a performance management system that includes regular feedback, coaching, and recognition.

REFLECTIONS

5

FINANCIAL MANAGEMENT AND PLANNING

Having your financials in order is an absolute must for running a successful business. After all, without money, it's impossible to keep a business afloat. It's surprisingly easy to end up bankrupt if you don't plan and manage your finances properly. From the very beginning, it's crucial to make informed decisions about the financial requirements of starting and sustaining your business. You need to ask yourself if your business will survive and thrive, and understand the costs associated with getting it off the ground and keeping it running.

Sometimes, people make the mistake of trying to expand their business prematurely. They might be barely getting by with their first location, yet they believe that opening a second location or franchising will solve their financial problems. However, it's important to remember that bigger doesn't always mean better. If you're already struggling financially and running a business in the red, trying to expand will only exacerbate the issues. Acting impulsively won't fix an already failing business.

To avoid these pitfalls, it's crucial to take charge of your finances, keep accurate records, and regularly assess the financial health of your business. If needed, seek guidance from financial professionals and create a realistic and sustainable financial plan. By doing so, you can ensure that your business remains financially stable and has the best chance of success and growth in the long run.

It's important to seek the necessary support and expertise when it comes to managing your business finances. Consider hiring professionals like bookkeepers, certified public accountants (CPAs), or other financial experts, especially those specializing in business finances. Not everyone possesses a natural aptitude for handling money or understanding credit. Credit is crucial for acquiring locations, setting up vendors, and securing necessary resources. Whether it's funds for equipment, supplies, rent or mortgage payments, vendor payments, or payroll, having a solid financial foundation is essential.

To ensure stability and promote growth, you must have a clear understanding of your financial health. Can you afford to hire more employees? Can you introduce new product lines or expand your services? Do you have more debt than you can handle? What is the state of your cash flow? It's important to assess these aspects to make informed business decisions. Additionally, it's crucial to evaluate the return on investment for any expensive masterminds or programs and ensure you will be able to take away information to help with your business growth and your development. Don't get pressured into signing up into every program because not every program is for everyone.

Researching industry standards can provide valuable insights into standard costs, such as food costs, average rent, and employee salaries. Understanding where you source your goods and how your pricing compares to competitors is also essential. By staying informed about these factors, you can make strategic decisions when it comes to managing your finances and positioning your business in the market.

Remember, seeking the support of financial professionals and staying informed about financial aspects specific to your industry can greatly contribute to the success and sustainability of your business.

Let me detail my own experience with finances.

As a business owner, it's crucial for me to prioritize fair and competitive compensation for my staff. However, to make informed decisions about pay rates, hiring new employees, purchasing products, or expanding, I understand the importance of knowing my monthly revenue and having a clear forecast for the next one, three, or even five years. This is especially important considering the recent rise in food costs, affecting prices at restaurants and even fast-food chains. In my case, as a childcare provider, I also need to factor in the expenses of providing meals and snacks for the children.

To ensure financial stability, I believe in running my business based on solid data and avoiding impulsive decisions driven by fear or wishful thinking. By understanding my numbers and having a reliable system in place, I can make sound financial choices. Rather than spending every dollar on personal desires like vacations, I prioritize reinvesting in the business. This approach allows me to allocate resources strategically and maintain long-term sustainability.

By knowing my long-term plan and regularly reviewing my financial situation, I can assess where I stand and make informed decisions. It's important to recognize that success in business requires more than just hoping for better circumstances tomorrow. It necessitates careful financial forecasting, understanding the market, managing costs effectively, and continuously reinvesting in the business. These practices not only help cover rising costs but also position my business for long-term growth and stability.

One crucial thing to always remember is to never mix personal and business funds. It's vital to keep them separate and avoid comingling of money. If you start using business funds for personal expenses, it can create a big mess, legally, and your accountant will have a hard time dealing with it. This is even more important for non-profit organizations, as they can lose their non-profit status if they don't handle their accounting carefully. Being organized is key when it comes to managing your business finances.

It's important to understand that what works for my business may not work for others. Each business is unique, and just because you see someone else doing something doesn't mean it will work for you too. You have to carve your own path and find what works best for your business. The most important thing is to plan ahead before you launch, seek help with managing your finances, and stay vigilant.

Establishing good financial management practices is crucial for the sustainability and growth of your business. Keep accurate records, track important financial metrics, and create realistic budgets. Regularly review your financial situation and make informed decisions based on the data you have. By doing so, you can ensure that your business finances are in order and set yourself up for success in the long run.

Implementing a robust accounting system is crucial for accurately tracking income, expenses, and cash flow, while developing financial projections and conducting regular budget reviews can help ensure financial stability and informed decision-making. Setting up key performance indicators (KPIs) to monitor financial health and regularly reviewing and updating your budget are also essential for aligning with business goals and revenue projections.

REGULARLY REVIEW AND UPDATE YOUR BUDGET:

Set up chart of accounts and categories to accurately track different types of income and expenses. Conduct regular budget reviews to compare actual financial performance against projections, identify variances, and make necessary adjustments to the budget.

Use these KPIs to assess performance, identify trends, and make data-driven decisions to improve financial stability.

Update the budget to reflect changes in the business environment, such as shifts in market conditions, changes in expenses, or unexpected opportunities or challenges.

ACTIONABLE ITEMS
TO PUT INTO PLACE

[X] Choosing an accounting software that fits the needs of your business insurance. It can handle income and expense, tracking, invoicing, payroll, and financial reporting.

[X] Regularly reconciled account, including bank statements to ensure accuracy and identify any discrepancies.

[X] Identify key financial KPI's, such as gross profit margin net profit margin current ratio in that to equity ratio to monitor the financial health of the business.

[X] Develop detailed financial projections, including sales, forecasting, expense, estimates, and cash flow projections for the short and long-term.

[X] Review your budget regularly to ensure it aligns with your business goals and revenue projections.

REFLECTIONS

6

MARKETING AND BRANDING

Brand awareness holds immense importance in the business world. It serves as your unique signature, encompassing elements such as your logo, colors, and messaging. Establishing a strong brand presence is essential because recognition is key. Just think about iconic brands like McDonald's—their recognizable golden arches and vibrant red color were the result of careful planning and strategy. Similarly, Starbucks can be identified instantly through its logo and distinctive green color, even without needing to read the word.

Building a successful brand goes beyond visual aspects. It involves creating a brand identity that resonates with your target audience. Take the example of Chick-fil-A, a billion-dollar company known for its distinct approach. By choosing to remain closed on Sundays and honoring the Sabbath, they showcase their values and respect for their employees' guaranteed day off. This decision appeals to a significant demographic of people who share similar beliefs. It's a unique aspect of their brand that sets them apart and establishes a strong connection with their target market.

In summary, brand awareness plays a crucial role in shaping how your business is perceived. By carefully planning and consistently delivering on your brand promise, you can create a memorable identity that resonates with your customers. This, in turn, fosters loyalty, customer engagement, and ultimately drives business success.

Employee uniforms and signage play a significant role in brand awareness and representation. When it comes to my business, I believe that uniforms should reflect our brand and create a visual connection between our employees and what we stand for. It's important for them to align with our logo, colors, and overall brand aesthetic.

Similarly, signage is a key element in catching the attention of potential customers and conveying our brand message. It should be eye-catching, large enough to be seen from the road, and strategically placed. The fonts used should be easily readable, ensuring that anyone passing by can quickly understand what our business is about. Effective signage should make it easy for people to recognize our business and grasp our offerings at a glance.

In today's digital world, brand consistency across online platforms is just as crucial. Our website should be user-friendly, with a clean and attractive design. It should be easy to navigate, with clear messaging that reflects our value proposition and mission. Our brand identity should be prominently displayed on the homepage, allowing visitors to immediately recognize who we are and what we offer. This consistency should extend to our presence on social media platforms such as Facebook, Instagram, LinkedIn, and others. When someone visits our website or social media profiles, they should be able to easily identify that they are engaging with our business. This alignment of branding should also be reflected in all our printed marketing materials.

By paying attention to these branding details and ensuring consistency across employee uniforms, signage, online platforms, and marketing materials, we create a strong and cohesive brand identity. This fosters brand awareness and makes it easier for people to recognize and connect with our business.

Color choice is an important aspect of psychology that has been studied extensively. Different colors have the power to evoke various emotions and feelings in people. It's crucial to consider color combinations because not all colors work well together and can either be pleasing or unpleasant to the eye. To effectively attract the clients you're targeting, it's advisable to seek the expertise of someone who understands this science and can determine the best colors for your business.

When it comes to marketing your business, it's worth exploring different avenues. If you operate locally, you might consider employing direct marketing strategies such as using car magnets. This approach works particularly well for service-based businesses like plumbing, contracting or electrical services, but it can be beneficial for almost any local business. By displaying your sign on your vehicle as you drive around, people will see it and may even take a picture of it on their phones for future reference or to share with someone they know might need your services.

Another example is how lawyers often place billboards on highways where accidents are likely to occur. This way, when people have an accident, they are more likely to remember or even see the billboards. To enhance the effectiveness of these marketing materials, incorporating QR codes can be helpful. QR codes allow people to quickly access relevant information by scanning the code with their smartphones.

It's essential to make it as easy as possible for people to find and reach out to you. One effective way to achieve this is by obtaining a phone number that is simple and memorable, and including it on all your marketing materials along with other contact methods like email. By providing easily accessible contact information, you remove barriers for people who want to connect with you and increase the likelihood of receiving inquiries.

Consistency in branding is also crucial. Avoid changing your brand frequently as it can lead to confusion and dilute your brand recognition. Maintain a consistent visual identity across various platforms and marketing materials. Additionally, it's important to establish a regular presence on social media platforms. Consistent posting helps to keep your brand visible and engaged with your audience. The same principle applies to blogs and newsletters—consistency is key. Develop a schedule for posting content and stick to it, rather than publishing sporadically.

To effectively market to your target audience, it's crucial to identify where they are most active on social media platforms. Understand which platforms your target audience prefers and focus your marketing efforts there. Technology is constantly evolving, and it's important to embrace and adapt to these changes. In today's digital landscape, it's necessary to have a presence across multiple platforms and engage in various marketing activities. Consistently posting content every day of the week and monitoring what your audience is looking for can help you tailor your approach and provide the content they desire.

Interactivity and fun play an important role in engaging your audience. Encourage interaction by responding to comments and messages promptly. Join relevant groups or communities where you can showcase your services and expertise. It's crucial to address negative comments or feedback as well. Apologize for any shortcomings and ask how you can rectify the situation. Demonstrating a willingness to listen and find solutions can help rebuild trust and maintain a positive brand image.

Customer relationships are a crucial part of your brand and how you respond to customers reflects your business's identity. The way you handle interactions can leave a lasting impression on people. While it's impossible to please everyone, it's important to respond to customer inquiries and feedback in a timely and respectful manner. Instead of getting angry or combative, approach customer interactions with a willingness to address concerns and seek a second chance. Embrace feedback as an opportunity to learn and improve.

Customer service is a vital aspect of your business. If there are complaints or dissatisfaction regarding customer service, take the time to understand the reasons behind them. If you claim to provide amazing customer service, ensure that it rings true in practice. Consistently strive to enhance the customer experience and exceed their expectations.

If you find yourself struggling with social media management, website upkeep, or overall marketing efforts due to lack of skills or time, consider hiring someone with expertise in these areas. Outsourcing these tasks to professionals can help ensure that your online presence remains active and engaging, and that your marketing efforts align with your business goals.

Marketing and branding are essential for attracting and retaining customers. Develop a comprehensive marketing strategy that encompasses various tactics to increase brand awareness. Clearly define your brand identity, including your values, personality, and positioning in the market. Utilize a mix of traditional and digital marketing channels to reach your target audience effectively. Regularly monitor and evaluate the effectiveness of your marketing campaigns to make informed decisions and optimize your strategy.

Remember, building strong customer relationships, delivering exceptional service, and consistently reinforcing your brand identity are key elements in fostering long-term success for your business.

ACTIONABLE ITEMS
TO PUT INTO PLACE

- ☒ Develop a content marketing strategy that provides valuable information to your target audience.

- ☒ Leverage social media platforms to engage with your customers, respond to inquiries, and share relevant content.

- ☒ Monitor and measure the effectiveness of your marketing campaigns using analytics tools and adjust your strategies accordingly.

- ☒ Implement a customer relationship management (CRM) system to better track customer interactions and preferences.

- ☒ Create personalized customer loyalty programs or incentives to reward repeat business and referrals.

REFLECTIONS

7

OPERATIONS AND EFFICIENCY WITH IMPLEMENTING (SOPS) STANDARD OPERATING PROCEDURES

Having clearly defined standards for our operations and processes is crucial for running our business efficiently. It's important that we know our Key Performance Indicators (KPIs) and ensure that our team leaders, directors, and managers are well-versed in them. They should be able to teach our staff how to follow our processes effectively.

I implemented a "score card." I offer bonuses for employees if they master specific KPIs. They can earn extra pay if they are in compliance with their employee handbook and in state compliance. We consider things like the cleanliness of their classrooms, whether or not they get to work on time, and their interactions with the students. Not everyone gives 100 percent on the job, but if you put a plan in place, your staff will know what you expect of them to earn more and grow into bigger, higher positions if they choose to climb the ladder.

In our business, for example, we have created step-by-step instructions on how to open up our school in the morning. This way, our staff can refer to the KPI and know exactly what to do. It provides clear guidance on getting the school ready and opening it for our students.

It's essential to have procedures in place for each important aspect of our business. If something were to happen to me, we need to ensure that the business can continue running smoothly. That's why having well-defined KPIs and Standard Operating Procedures (SOPs) is crucial. They provide the framework for how tasks should be executed, regardless of who is in charge.

We should also consider streamlining our processes to make them more efficient. It's important to take the time to understand how our team members learn best. Not everyone enjoys reading lengthy text in a binder. Some people may prefer videos, audio recordings, or graphics. By catering to different learning preferences, such as using visual aids or interactive materials, we can improve comprehension and ensure that everyone understands and follows our processes effectively.

Upon analyzing our onboarding Key Performance Indicator (KPI), we discovered that it wasn't yielding the desired results. Despite conducting eight hours of training sessions, our staff struggled to retain the information we imparted to them. This made me reflect on my own college experiences. Let's be honest, how much do we truly remember from all those years of studying? Personally, it wasn't until I started working hands-on with patients, performing tasks like blood work and checking blood pressure, that the processes truly sank in. Real-life experience was the catalyst for remembering and applying what I had learned. It was like riding a bike—it all came back to me.

It's essential to present the information our staff needs to know in ways that they can understand and retain. If we fail to do so, we'll end up shouldering all the responsibilities ourselves. A prime example is the restaurant industry. They utilize par sheets to determine how much they need to order based on past performance averages, both weekly and across different seasons. This data-driven approach ensures that they have the necessary supplies and ingredients to meet customer demand.

By considering the effectiveness of our training methods and finding ways to make the information more relatable and memorable, we can equip our staff with the tools they need to succeed in all aspects of our business procedures. It's important to create an environment that nurtures on-the-job learning and provides opportunities for practical application, just like my experience in nursing. This way, our staff will be better prepared to handle real-life situations and contribute to the success of our business.

I believe it's crucial for businesses to prioritize inventory management to avoid unnecessary expenses and improve efficiency. Many businesses, including restaurants, bars, and childcare centers, often face challenges related to supply needs. Overbuying or underbuying can lead to wastage or running out of essential items, which can negatively impact customer confidence and overall operations.

To tackle these issues, it's important to conduct regular inventory counts and create par sheets for all items. This helps in establishing minimum stock levels and ensures timely reordering. Additionally, leveraging inventory management software can streamline the process by tracking stock levels, generating reports, and automating reordering tasks.

Building strong relationships with reliable suppliers is also crucial. By working closely with them, businesses can ensure timely deliveries and negotiate favorable pricing and terms for bulk purchases. Monitoring sales and demand patterns enables businesses to adjust inventory levels accordingly, avoiding overstocking or understocking.

Minimizing waste is another key aspect. For instance, in the case of restaurants, if a particular dish isn't selling well, offering it as a special can help prevent food waste before resorting to disposal. Similarly, childcare centers can save costs by purchasing snacks and supplies in bulk from wholesale stores like Sam's or Costco instead of buying them at higher prices from nearby supermarkets or corner stores.

Centralizing inventory management, especially for businesses with multiple locations or departments, can optimize stock levels and prevent duplication of purchases. It's important to provide proper training and education to staff members so they understand the significance of inventory management and follow the correct procedures for receiving, storing, and tracking inventory.

By implementing these strategies, businesses can maintain optimal inventory levels, reduce waste, and improve overall operations while also saving money in the long run.

It's important to regularly revisit and reassess your business processes and procedures to identify areas for improvement. Embracing technology can be a game-changer, especially with the availability of Customer Relationship Management (CRM) systems.

CRMs offer various benefits, such as acquiring new clients through mass email blasts and targeted campaigns. Even when I don't have immediate availability for new students, I make sure to keep in touch with interested families, letting them know they are still on my radar and that I'll reach out as soon as a spot opens up. Surveys are a great way to gather feedback from clients, asking questions like "How can we improve?" or "What else do you need from us?" This valuable feedback helps identify opportunities to enhance our services and address customer needs.

I find it helpful to create and maintain Excel sheets to track and analyze different aspects of my business. Regularly reviewing and updating these sheets ensures I have the most accurate and current data to inform my decision-making process.

Furthermore, there are numerous apps available that can assist in measuring and improving various aspects of your business. Whether it's productivity tools or analytics platforms, these apps offer valuable insights that can streamline operations and drive growth.

Remaining open-minded and receptive to new ideas and tools is vital for the success of your business. By combining a willingness to embrace technology with a deep understanding of your processes and procedures, you can continuously improve and achieve greater success while keeping your customers satisfied.

Efficient operations are key to achieving profitability and customer satisfaction.

IMPLEMENT A CLOUD-BASED PLATFORM:

Transitioning to a cloud-based platform can streamline processes and make operations more efficient by enabling remote access, improving scalability, and enhancing collaboration. It can also lead to cost savings in the long run by reducing the need for physical infrastructure and maintenance.

SET UP KEY PERFORMANCE INDICATORS (KPIS):

Establishing KPIs is crucial for monitoring the operation and efficiency of the business. KPIs provide measurable targets and benchmarks that can be used to track performance and identify areas for improvement. Examples of KPIs include customer acquisition cost, customer retention rate, production yield, and service response time.

ENCOURAGE CROSS-DEPARTMENTAL:

Encourage collaboration. Regular knowledge-sharing sessions or workshops can foster collaboration and information exchange across different departments. This can lead to improved problem-solving, innovation, and efficiency by leveraging the diverse expertise within the organization.

ESTABLISH AN INNOVATION TASK FORCE OR COMMITTEE:

Creating a dedicated team or committee focused on driving innovation initiatives can help the business stay competitive and adapt to changing market conditions. The task force can be responsible for identifying new opportunities, evaluating emerging technologies, and implementing innovative solutions to improve processes and products.

IMPLEMENT CONTINUOUS IMPROVEMENT:

Create processes. Foster a culture of continuous improvement by implementing processes such as Six Sigma, Lean Management, or Kaizen. These methodologies focus on identifying and eliminating waste, streamlining processes, and optimizing operations to achieve higher efficiency and quality.

ACTIONABLE ITEMS
TO PUT INTO PLACE

Here are five actionable items to put into place to improve the operation and efficiency of a business:

- ☒ Implementing a CRM system which can streamline operations, improve efficiency, and enhance customer relationships by centralizing customer data, automating tasks, improving communication, providing insights, and optimizing customer service.

- ☒ Implement lean principles for continuous improvement.

- ☒ Investing in technology to automate tasks and improve communication and business operations can significantly enhance efficiency, productivity, and overall performance of your organization.

- ☒ Monitor key performance indicators (KPIs) to track performance and drive improvement.

- ☒ Provide continuance employee training and development opportunities.

REFLECTIONS

8

CUSTOMER RELATIONSHIP MANAGEMENT INNOVATION, QUALITY, AND EFFICIENCY

Obtaining customers or clients is the first part of the equation when launching or growing a business. Your marketing plan should include ways to reach your potential customers but you must also consider ways to manage the relationship between your business and that customer. Being innovative is one way to attract and keep customers.

For instance, during the COVID-19 pandemic, ensuring the safety of students and staff in schools became a top priority. This led to a deeper consideration of cleanliness and innovative solutions. Many schools installed misters at their entrances, which sprayed a safe yet effective solution to kill bacteria on contact. Additionally, they used machines to disinfect toys by heating them to about 150 degrees, effectively eliminating all bacteria. Each classroom was assigned a specific time to bring their toys for disinfection. These innovations aimed to better serve the staff and children, ultimately creating a safer environment. Such initiatives represent innovation and demonstrate the importance of thinking outside the box to address critical needs.

When it comes to running a business, getting customers on board is just the first step. It's equally important to manage the relationship between your business and those customers. That's where your marketing plan comes in. It should not only focus on ways to reach potential customers but also consider how to nurture and maintain those relationships. And one effective way to do that is through innovation.

These innovations not only helped us address the challenges posed by the pandemic but also strengthened our relationship with our students and their families. By taking proactive measures to enhance cleanliness and safety, we demonstrate our commitment to quality and efficiency.

Innovation doesn't have to be complicated—it can be as simple as rethinking a classic menu item at a restaurant. By doing something interesting like putting the cheese inside the cheeseburger, instead of on top, the eatery can add an exciting element to the dish and make it more memorable. It shows your restaurant thinks outside the box and pays attention to the little details, which can leave a lasting impression. In addition, you can set yourself apart by creating your own unique sauces or offering a cocktail menu with unexpected twists. Developing signature sauces that are exclusive to your restaurant adds a special touch to your dishes, making them stand out from the competition. Similarly, incorporating fresh herbs or using smoking techniques in your cocktails can provide a unique and memorable drinking experience for your customers.

By being different and embracing creativity, you can attract new customers and keep them coming back for more. When people encounter something innovative and exciting in your menu, they are more likely to be intrigued and eager to return. It's the element of surprise and originality that keeps customers engaged and coming back for the innovative experiences you offer.

Amazon has a unique and innovative policy that sets them apart in the retail industry—they offer free returns. Unlike local shops or boutiques where purchases are typically non-refundable, Amazon allows customers to return items even if they simply don't like what they bought. This decision was not required of them, but they chose to implement it to become leaders in retail sales.

Innovation plays a significant role in providing a higher level of service. For example, if you own a brick and mortar clothing boutique, you can think creatively to offer additional services that differentiate you from the competition. One idea is to partner with a local seamstress who can provide alteration services. This could be a stay-at-home mom or a retired person who has a passion for sewing and would appreciate the extra work. By collaborating with them, you not only support someone in need of employment but also offer your clients an extra level of service.

Having a seamstress available means that your customers can have their purchased clothing items tailored to their specific measurements and preferences. This personalized approach goes beyond the standard one-size-fits-all mentality and enhances the overall shopping experience. It shows that your boutique is committed to customer satisfaction and willing to go the extra mile.

By incorporating this innovative service, you can attract more customers and increase sales. Knowing they have the option to have their clothes altered to fit them perfectly gives them confidence in their purchase. It sets your boutique apart from others and builds customer loyalty by offering convenience and customization.

Adding a new skill can bring innovation and efficiency to your work. As a graphic designer, for example, learning how to make websites can strengthen your relationship with clients and increase your income through referrals. The key is to differentiate yourself and put your own twist on things. Don't just do what everyone else is doing.

Coaching, on the other hand, is facing some challenges due to the abundance of coaches in popular fields like confidence, weight loss, relationships, or anxiety. When everyone teaches the same thing, it's hard to stand out and be innovative. That's why specificity is crucial. Find your area of expertise and approach coaching in a unique way that sets you apart from the competition. Trying to teach the same thing with the same parameters as others means you'll have a lot of competition.

One way to do this is by focusing on new technologies such as AI or business building. By offering coaching on these emerging topics, you can provide a fresh and innovative approach. Teach people how to utilize AI effectively or guide them in building successful businesses. Emphasize practical application, provide personalized strategies, and stay updated with the latest trends to offer valuable insights to your clients.

Remember to highlight the importance of human skills alongside AI. Show how technology can enhance rather than replace human capabilities. Creating a collaborative community or networking platform where your clients can connect and learn from each other is also a great way to add value to your coaching services. By being different and offering a unique perspective, you can set yourself apart in the coaching industry.

Quality is a crucial factor in building strong relationships with customers. When it comes to restaurants, using high-quality products like Wagyu beef, fresh farm-to-table vegetables and meats, or locally caught fish creates a perception of offering the best food quality.

Maintaining cleanliness is also essential in reflecting the overall quality of a business. Both the environment and the employees should be clean and presentable. The way your staff interacts with customers is another aspect that contributes to the overall quality experience. Being better than the competition often boils down to providing better quality in various aspects.

Having a well-trained staff, ensuring a clean environment, using superior ingredients for your food, and opting for safer chemicals for pest control or laundry services are all examples of how quality matters.

A great example of a company that understands the importance of quality is Costco. They don't carry every brand available, but they carefully select products based on their quality standards. When you buy electronics—like a TV—from Costco, you won't find a hundred different brands to choose from. Instead, they offer choices that have been thoroughly researched and determined to provide the best quality at the best price.

Efficiency is key when it comes to reaching out and staying in contact with customers. Technology is constantly evolving and improving, and by embracing these changes, you can be innovative and efficient in your approach.

In our business, we utilize technology to streamline our operations and improve efficiency. On our website, we have simple forms that capture important customer data. We ask for their name, email address, and phone number, which is directly stored in our Customer Relationship Management system (CRM) database. This allows us to easily follow up with potential clients using automatic responders through an app called Chat Bolt. When someone fills out the form, they receive an email from us, and we also receive a notification. This enables us to promptly respond to inquiries, schedule school tours, or address any questions.

You may have noticed similar technology being used on social media platforms. For example, when you click on an ad, you often receive a private message asking how they can assist you with your purchase or provide information.

By leveraging technology effectively, we can efficiently manage customer communication and save time. It allows us to provide timely and personalized responses, enhancing the overall customer experience.

Restaurants often use reservation systems to capture customer information, not only for managing reservations but also to stay connected with their patrons. They can use this information to keep customers informed about promotions, events, new fragrances, seasonal products, or sales. The aim is to stay top of mind and ensure customers don't miss out on anything exciting.

I personally receive regular reminders from Bath and Body Works and Starbucks. Bath and Body Works informs me about sales, new fragrances, and seasonal products, while Starbucks announces the arrival of seasonal flavors and delicious baked goods. Even if the messages can sometimes feel overwhelming, I hesitate to unsubscribe because I don't want to miss out on any updates or offers.

Research suggests that it takes about seven interactions for the average person to engage with a business. Simply posting once on social media or running an ad doesn't guarantee reaching the target customers effectively. It's important to have multiple touchpoints to capture their attention and maintain engagement.

Surveys are also an efficient way to gather customer feedback and improve customer relationships. Restaurants often provide surveys that customers can fill out when paying the bill. This feedback allows businesses to identify areas for improvement and make necessary changes. Being open to criticism and actively working on making improvements is key.

By utilizing reservation systems, keeping customers informed through targeted messaging, and actively seeking feedback, businesses can enhance customer engagement and build stronger relationships.

I recently became a realtor and added it to my business skill set. I truly understand the importance of maintaining high standards and ethical conduct in all my dealings with clients. It's not just about representing myself well, but also about upholding the reputation of my brokerage. That's why I believe in continual training to ensure I know what is expected of me when working with clients and customers.

To enhance customer engagement and build stronger relationships, I implemented various strategies. First, I set up a reservation system that allows clients to conveniently schedule appointments or property viewings. This reduces wait times and enhances the overall customer experience.

Additionally, I use targeted messaging techniques to keep my customers informed. Through personalized emails, SMS notifications, and newsletters, I provide valuable and timely information about new property listings, market updates, and other relevant details. This helps me stay connected with my clients and engage them effectively.

Feedback from clients is crucial for improvement. I actively seek feedback through surveys, online reviews, and personal follow-ups. By listening to my clients' needs, preferences, and concerns, I can address any issues and demonstrate my commitment to their satisfaction.

I have also invested in training programs to ensure my staff is well-prepared and knowledgeable. This includes educating them on ethical standards, company policies, and customer service skills. It is essential my team understands the expectations and responsibilities when working with clients, including maintaining confidentiality, providing accurate information, and acting in the client's best interest.

I highly believe in learning and professional development. I encourage my team to attend industry conferences, participate in training programs, and obtain relevant certifications. By staying updated with industry trends and best practices, we ensure that we are providing the best service to our clients.

By implementing these strategies, I aim to enhance customer engagement, build trust and loyalty, and differentiate my brokerage in a competitive market.

Building strong relationships with your customers is crucial for long-term success. Provide excellent customer service and prioritize customer satisfaction. Implement a customer relationship management (CRM) system to track customer interactions, gather feedback, and personalize the customer experience. Actively listen to your customers, address their concerns promptly, and continuously seek ways to improve their experience with your business.

ACTIONABLE ITEMS
TO PUT INTO PLACE

☒ Implement a CRM system to track customer interactions, preferences, and purchase history.

☒ Develop personalized marketing and communication strategies based on customer segmentation and behavior.

☒ Proactively seek customer feedback through surveys, reviews, and social media to identify areas for improvement.

☒ Conduct regular performance evaluations and provide constructive feedback to help employees grow and develop.

☒ Implement a recognition and rewards program to acknowledge and appreciate employee achievements.

REFLECTIONS

9

HUMAN RESOURCES AND TALENT MANAGEMENT

A skilled and motivated workforce is essential for business success. This pillar discusses the importance of effective recruitment, employee training and development, performance management, fostering a positive work environment, and implementing fair compensation and benefits.

A strong human resources department (HR) is crucial for any business or organization to be successful. This is where you convey your policies, procedures, and practices. Human resources are there to protect your business liability from lawsuits, to handle the workforce, hire, train and retain staff, attract, develop, and motivate them. HR helps your business comply with labor laws and state and federal regulations.

There is a federal minimum wage and each state must meet that minimum, but some states offer a higher rate. HR will make sure the business is in compliance and that overtime wages and anything to do with employee hours are dealt with.

It is common knowledge that many businesses in America are experiencing a shortage of staff. Post-pandemic, it has become more a matter of what the employer offers employees and not what the candidate for employment brings to the table. Employees are seeking things like flexible schedules, increased pay rates, and part time instead of full time work. Some prefer four 10-hour days or to work only in the mornings or afternoons. In my childcare business, we have learned to adapt to this. Sometimes we hire two part-time people to fill one full-time position. We have to accommodate our staff's needs as we cannot run a school without competent staff. To get the best people for the job, we need to be flexible. I have over-hired at times. Yes, this can be costly but by having extra staff we know we can cover sick days and incidents that occur.

The hospitality industry is suffering staff shortages more than some other industries. Times to check in are often later while waiting for the smaller staff to clean the rooms. Sometimes housekeeping only offers additional towels and paper products rather than cleaning during stays

There are far more subcontractors, 1099 employees, now than there have ever been. They work at their own pace and can do more of what they want. W-2 employees have more rules of conduct and expectations. HR is the steward of those expectations. With subcontractors, it is a bit harder to monitor their day to day work but rather just a matter of setting tasks and the expected results. There are benefits of hiring 1099 employees. Payroll tax is expensive and workers compensation is extremely costly. If you have employees working on site at your business, you MUST have workers comp! One accident—one person slips and falls—and you don't have workers comp and you are in serious trouble. You can lose your entire business and possibly your personal assets. Before you start your business, make sure this is in place.

Insurance is equally important. Don't open your doors or even start your build out without having insurance in place. If there is fire or hurricane, any accident or act of God, and you don't have insurance, you could lose everything.

We are often in a rush to hire people. But they need to be the right people for the job. When they are hired, you must then have a plan to onboard them and send them through orientation and training. Throwing people into work positions who are not properly onboarded and trained is a recipe for disaster.

HR fosters positive relationships between staff and management, between worker to worker, and manager to manager. Managers who are not treating staff with respect will find themselves at HR, where they the HR manager will help clear the air, hear the grievances, and correct any bad behavior.

Harassment issues can ruin a business. The appropriate way to act and speak in the workplace must be made extremely clear to all members of the organization. There may need to be mediation to ensure a healthy work environment. People have personal lives and personal issues which can affect how they are acting at work. HR needs to be on hand to evaluate employee performance. We need people to run a business, but you have to have the right people in the right seat on the bus. Personality and personal issues need to be left at the door when coming to work. Sometimes, an employee is in the wrong position and moving him or her can affect positive changes. Other times, they are not right for the company and must be let go. Without an HR person to handle those issues, things can lead to legal issues, lawsuits, and other problems.

It is important for any business to hold people accountable and to set certain standards that must be met. If there are sales quotas, those have to be met. If there are complaints from customers, those need to be addressed with the employee in question and corrected. Performance evaluations can make that clear and can allow HR to do their job well. They can retrain and educate the person who is falling short.

HR can help create training and continuing education, identify training needs, and create training programs. Your business is not a hobby if you want to be successful, no matter how big or small the business is or plans to be.

We also conduct an exit interview when an employee leaves our organization. Employees are asked to fill out a survey. This helps us improve the business as leaders. If you can't retain employees, you are likely the problem, not them. In some cases not everyone is fit for particular jobs which is okay but helps us identify the gap and put the correct people in the correct seats. You might want to also look at what you could be doing wrong. Don't feel discouraged, use it as a guide, go back to the drawing board and see what could be going wrong. You will also want to look at if you have a poor work environment, low pay, lack of respect from management, or poor morale? You will want to find out what the issue is, and fix it immediately.

I strongly believe that people thrive when they feel appreciated and valued in their work. When you show your employees you appreciate their efforts and acknowledge their importance, they become motivated to go above and beyond for you. It's amazing how much people are willing to do for less if they are genuinely happy in their jobs and feel a sense of belonging to the company.

The nature of the workforce has changed significantly in recent times. One hiring model that has caught my attention is the one implemented by Chick-fil-A. Their employees are incredibly diligent and hardworking, even when they have to stand outside in their uniforms for hours, taking orders from the carline. What strikes me the most is that they seem genuinely happy in their jobs. I believe this is a result of Chick-fil-A's focus on building a strong company culture. By prioritizing their employees' well-being and creating a positive work environment, they have achieved a workforce that consistently delivers exceptional customer service.

Another example that comes to mind is the employees at Disney World. Despite having to walk around the park in costumes in scorching 100-degree weather, they still appear happy and dedicated to their work. I like to think that this is because they feel valued and appreciated by the company. Being in an environment filled with music and happiness likely contributes to their overall job satisfaction.

It is essential to appreciate and value your employees if you want to maintain a motivated and dedicated workforce. The examples of Chick-fil-A and Disney World demonstrate the power of creating a positive company culture where employees feel valued and part of something meaningful. By fostering an environment of appreciation and recognition, you can enhance job satisfaction, loyalty, and customer service.

ACTIONABLE ITEMS
TO PUT INTO PLACE

☒ Foster a culture of experimentation and risk-taking by encouraging employees to generate and test new ideas.

☒ Regularly assess your business processes and identify opportunities for automation or optimization.

☒ Stay informed about emerging technologies, industry trends, and competitor strategies to identify potential disruptions and adapt accordingly.

☒ Develop a code of conduct that outlines ethical guidelines for all employees to follow.

☒ Provide ethics training to ensure employees understand the importance of ethical behavior in the workplace.

REFLECTIONS

10

CONTINUOUS LEARNING AND ADAPTABILITY

In a rapidly changing business landscape, the ability to learn and adapt is essential. This pillar explores the importance of fostering a culture of continuous learning, embracing innovation, monitoring industry trends, and being open to change and adaptation. Monitor market trends and embrace technological advancements that can enhance your business operations. Foster a culture of innovation by encouraging creativity and risk-taking. Encourage employees to generate new ideas, and provide them with the resources and support to implement innovative solutions. By staying ahead of the curve, you can seize new opportunities and better respond to market shifts.

As someone working in a service industry, such as massage therapy, real estate, chiropractic care, or teaching, I understand the importance of being a lifelong learner. Continuing education is a vital aspect of these professions, and it's crucial to embrace the need for ongoing learning if we want to grow and succeed.

Personally, I am committed to never stop learning. I've experienced tremendous business growth by actively seeking mentorship and engaging in professional development opportunities. Learning from individuals who have already faced the challenges I may encounter has been invaluable. Their guidance has helped me become a better leader and strengthened my business skills. I firmly believe that knowledge is power.

To further enhance my growth, I have sought out partnerships with individuals who have helped me scale my business more rapidly. I understand that sometimes, who you know is just as important as what you know. By investing in memberships to high-quality networking groups, I have been able to level up and expand my professional network. These connections have presented me with new opportunities and opened doors to success.

In today's digital age, it's easy to rely on Google for answers to everything. But let's face it, there are times when we need to seek help from experts to learn specific skills and figure out how to apply them effectively. The world is constantly changing, and it's essential to keep up with the newest advancements and innovations, especially in technology.

I firmly believe that if you do the same things in your business for 20 years, you'll get the same results. That's why I've embraced professional development as a way to accelerate my growth. It has truly been a game changer and has played a significant role in making me as successful as I am today.

Adaptability and a willingness to change are vital if you want your business to thrive and expand. Let's be honest, if you attend a training or take a course and end up with a notebook full of valuable notes that just sits on a shelf gathering dust, nothing will change. Implementation is key. We have to take action and apply the knowledge we've gained to see real results.

Once I determine the goal, I create a 100-day plan and my personal and business routine revolves around this. It helps me stay focused and organized. One of the key aspects of my plan is setting aside time each month to learn something new. I firmly believe that continuous learning makes us smarter and more capable. You get smarter when you learn. I make it a habit to write down my goals and revisit them frequently to stay on track.

Learn all the skills you can. If you can't afford a mentor right away, do an internship, watch videos, or take free or inexpensive online courses. You might not have the money for the mentor you seek, but you can partner with someone who can teach you things by offering your time to assist them on a project or in their business in trade for some education.

As a realtor, I understand the importance of continuing education. It's an ongoing requirement in my field, and I fully embrace it. Attending classes or training sessions without implementing the concepts and strategies learned would be a waste of time and effort. I believe in being proactive and applying what I learn to enhance my skills and improve my business. You have to be a go-getter.

Networking and connecting with people is another crucial aspect of personal and professional growth. I'm naturally shy, yet I push myself to step out of my comfort zone and engage with others. Building relationships and expanding my network is invaluable in this industry. You have to talk to people, reach out, and connect, even if you are shy (like I am).

I also believe in investing in the education of my staff. Encouraging them to learn and acquire skills that can contribute to our business growth is essential. I challenge my team members to share their knowledge with me and with each other. Get your staff to be excited and invested in education too. Have them learn things that will increase business, and challenge them to teach you things. You can't be everywhere all the time, but a well-trained staff can be your surrogate and can bring fresh ideas and perspectives to the workplace.

There's no need to feel ashamed if you don't succeed as a business owner. Closing a business doesn't make you a failure; instead, it offers valuable lessons for personal growth. The truth is, entrepreneurship isn't meant for everyone, and that's okay. It's worth considering if being an excellent employee might suit you better. After all, there's a high demand for exceptional employees, and many businesses would be thrilled to have you on their team.

Understanding ourselves and reflecting on your strengths and preferences can be challenging yet essential. It's important to ask yourself if you're truly prepared to put in the necessary work to be a successful business owner, or if you would be better off as an employee who genuinely cares about their work. If the latter resonates with you, there are numerous job opportunities available, and companies would be excited to welcome you aboard.

Recognizing your limitations and being willing to hire experts is a wise choice. We can't be expected to know or master everything. As a realtor, for instance, I decided to hire a Social Media Manager (SMM) who specializes in the industry. I understand the significance of reaching people through social media, but I personally lack the expertise in that area. By bringing in a skilled SMM who handles this aspect of the business on a daily basis, my life becomes easier, and it leads to quicker and greater success.

Planning for future growth is crucial. This might involve finding a mentor who can provide guidance and support or seeking additional resources to aid in personal and professional development. It's important to remember success doesn't always mean going it alone; it often involves building a team and leveraging the strengths of others.

Ultimately, the most important thing is to be honest with yourself and make choices that align with your strengths and aspirations. Whether you choose to pursue entrepreneurship or thrive as an exceptional employee, there are opportunities available to you. The key is to find the path that resonates with you and allows you to flourish.

ACTIONABLE ITEMS
TO PUT INTO PLACE

☒ Encourage employees to pursue professional development opportunities, such as online courses or industry certifications.

☒ Create a knowledge-sharing platform or organize regular team meetings to facilitate learning and cross-departmental collaboration.

☒ Regularly evaluate your business performance against key metrics and conduct post-project reviews to identify lessons learned and areas for improvement.

☒ Conduct a comprehensive risk assessment to identify potential risks and vulnerabilities.

☒ Develop a crisis management plan that outlines protocols for handling emergencies or unforeseen events.

REFLECTIONS

A SUMMARY OF THE PILLARS

Owning and operating a successful business requires a holistic approach that encompasses various critical pillars. By focusing on vision and strategic planning, market research, product development, effective leadership, financial management, marketing, operations, human resources, customer relationship management, and continuous learning, entrepreneurs can establish a solid foundation for their businesses. Each pillar contributes to the overall success and sustainability of the enterprise. By understanding and implementing these principles, entrepreneurs can navigate challenges, seize opportunities, and increase their chances of achieving long-term business success.

MORE WAYS TO IMPROVE YOUR BUSINESS

There are many important elements of running a successful business. I have expanded on each topic to help you gain the necessary knowledge.

THE IMPORTANCE OF CREATING SOPS

One of my biggest takeaways that changed my business is when we added Standard Operating Procedures (SOPs), which are a set of step-by-step instructions created by a business to help workers carry out complex routine operations. SOPs aim to achieve efficiency, quality output, and uniformity of performance, while reducing miscommunication and failure to comply with industry regulations.

WHY WE NEED STANDARD OPERATING PROCEDURES:

EFFICIENCY AND CONSISTENCY: SOPs ensure that business processes run more efficiently, which improves productivity. They also ensure that company operations are performed consistently every time, regardless of who is performing the task.

QUALITY CONTROL: SOPs help maintain the quality of output by providing workers with a detailed, consistent procedure to follow.

TRAINING TOOL: SOPs serve as an excellent training tool for new employees and for training existing employees on new procedures.

COMPLIANCE AND REGULATION: Many industries have strict operational and reporting procedures that need to be adhered to. SOPs can help ensure that these procedures are followed correctly, which can prevent legal and regulatory issues.

RISK REDUCTION: By providing clear instructions, SOPs can help reduce the risk of mishaps and mistakes, and ensure that work is performed safely and effectively.

CUSTOMER FOCUS: Always prioritize the needs of your customers. Regularly ask for their feedback to understand their needs and wants. This can help you to improve your products or services.

EMPLOYEE ENGAGEMENT: Engage employees by regularly communicating with them, listening to their ideas, and recognizing their work. Engaged employees are more productive and can help you to achieve your business goals.

EMBRACE TECHNOLOGY: Technology can help you streamline your operations, improve your products or services, and engage with your customers more effectively. Consider implementing a customer relationship management (CRM) system, using social media for marketing, or using analytics to understand your customers' behaviors.

CONTINUOUS IMPROVEMENT: Always look for ways to improve your business processes. This could involve simplifying processes, eliminating wasteful activities, or implementing new procedures.

FINANCIAL MANAGEMENT: Keep a close eye on your finances. Regularly review your costs and look for ways to reduce them without compromising on quality. Also, ensure that you have enough cash flow to cover your expenses.

STRATEGIC PLANNING: Have a clear vision for your business and set realistic goals. Regularly review your business strategy to ensure that you are on track to achieve your goals.

NETWORKING: Building relationships with other businesses can open up new opportunities. Attend networking events, join business associations, and look for ways to collaborate with other businesses.

Remember, every business is unique, so what works for one business may not work for another. It's important to experiment with different strategies and continually learn and adapt.

BUILDING ORGANIZATIONAL SKILLS

Organizational skills are crucial for owning and operating a successful business. Here's how organization ties in with running a successful business:

EFFICIENCY: Being organized helps improve efficiency in business operations. When you have systems and processes in place, tasks are streamlined, and employees know what needs to be done, where to find information, and how to prioritize their work. This reduces wasted time and improves productivity.

TIME MANAGEMENT: Effective organization helps you manage your time more efficiently. By planning and prioritizing tasks, you can allocate your time effectively and ensure important activities are not overlooked. This allows you to focus on strategic decision-making, business growth, and customer engagement.

RESOURCE ALLOCATION: Organizational skills help you allocate resources effectively. Whether it's managing finances, inventory, or human resources, being organized allows you to optimize resource allocation, reduce waste, and make informed decisions about budgeting and staffing.

CUSTOMER SERVICE: Organized businesses are better equipped to provide excellent customer service. By keeping track of customer information, purchase history, and preferences, you can personalize your interactions and anticipate customer needs. This leads to higher customer satisfaction and loyalty.

PLANNING AND GOAL SETTING: Organization is essential for effective planning and goal setting. By setting clear objectives, breaking them down into actionable steps, and creating timelines, you can map out your business's path to success. Being organized also allows you to monitor progress, identify bottlenecks, and make necessary adjustments to stay on track.

RISK MANAGEMENT: Organized businesses are better prepared to mitigate risks. By maintaining accurate records, implementing proper security measures, and having contingency plans in place, you can minimize the impact of potential risks, such as data breaches, supply chain disruptions, and legal issues.

DECISION MAKING: Organization provides you with the information and data needed to make informed decisions. When your business is well-organized, you have easy access to financial statements, sales reports, market research, and other key information. This allows you to analyze situations, identify trends, and make strategic decisions that drive business growth.

Overall, organization is a fundamental aspect of running a successful business. It enhances efficiency, improves time management, supports customer service, facilitates planning and goal setting, aids in resource allocation, strengthens risk management, and enables effective decision making. Investing time and effort into developing and maintaining organizational skills will yield significant benefits for your business.

ABI – ALWAYS BE IMPROVING

Businesses that do not improve their operations over time can face several challenges, including the following:

LOSS OF COMPETITIVE ADVANTAGE: If competitors are continually improving their operations and your business is not, that business may fall behind. This could result in loss of market share, decreased sales, and reduced profitability.

INEFFICIENCY: Without improvements, processes may become outdated and inefficient. This can lead to increased costs, decreased productivity, and lower quality products or services.

CUSTOMER DISSATISFACTION: Today's customers typically expect businesses to continually improve their products, services, and customer service. If a business does not meet these expectations, it may lose customers to competitors.

EMPLOYEE TURNOVER: Employees often want to work for companies that are innovative and continually improving. If a business is stagnating, it may have difficulty attracting and retaining talented employees.

DIFFICULTY ADAPTING TO CHANGES: The business world is continually changing, and businesses that do not improve their operations may have difficulty adapting to new technologies, market trends, and changes in consumer behavior.

REGULATORY COMPLIANCE ISSUES: In certain industries, businesses are required to update their operations to stay in compliance with changing regulations. Failure to do so can result in penalties, fines, and other legal consequences.

PROFITABILITY ISSUES: All of the above factors can lead to decreased profitability over time. If a business is not profitable, it may eventually have to close its doors.

In summary, continuous improvement is a key factor in the long-term success of a business. Businesses that do not prioritize improvement may face significant challenges and risks.

IMPROVING YOUR BUSINESS OPERATIONS

Businesses that make a concerted effort to improve their operations can experience several positive outcomes. Here are some potential results of improving business operations:

INCREASED EFFICIENCY AND PRODUCTIVITY: By identifying and eliminating bottlenecks, streamlining processes, and implementing best practices, businesses can significantly improve their efficiency and productivity. This leads to cost savings, faster turnaround times, and increased output without compromising quality.

ENHANCED CUSTOMER SATISFACTION: Improving operations often translates into better customer experiences. When businesses operate more efficiently, they can deliver products or services more quickly and accurately. This leads to improved customer satisfaction, increased loyalty, and positive word-of-mouth referrals.

COST REDUCTION: Operational improvements often result in cost savings. By optimizing processes, businesses can eliminate waste, reduce errors, and lower overhead expenses. This can include areas such as inventory management, supply chain optimization, and resource allocation.

Lowering costs can contribute to higher profit margins and increased competitiveness.

IMPROVED QUALITY AND CONSISTENCY: Operational improvements can lead to enhanced product or service quality and consistency. By implementing standardized procedures, quality control measures, and employee training programs, businesses can ensure their offerings meet or exceed customer expectations. This can lead to a stronger reputation and a competitive advantage in the market.

BETTER ADAPTABILITY AND AGILITY: Businesses that continuously improve their operations are more adaptable and agile in responding to market changes and customer demands. They can quickly identify emerging trends, capitalize on new opportunities, and navigate challenges more effectively. This flexibility allows businesses to stay ahead of the competition and remain relevant in rapidly changing environments.

EMPLOYEE ENGAGEMENT AND SATISFACTION: Operational improvements often involve optimizing workflows, providing better tools and resources, and empowering employees. This can result in increased employee engagement, satisfaction, and morale. When employees see that their suggestions are valued and their work environment supports efficiency, they are more likely to be motivated and committed to the business's success.

SCALABILITY AND GROWTH: Improved operations lay a foundation for scalability and growth. When businesses have streamlined processes, standardized procedures, and put efficient systems in place, they can easily scale their operations to meet increased demand. This allows them to pursue new markets, expand their customer base, and seize growth opportunities.

It's important to note that operational improvements require ongoing effort, monitoring, and adaptation. Businesses should continually assess their operations, gather feedback, and seek opportunities for further enhancements to sustain these positive outcomes over the long term.

SOME COMMON FACTORS FOR BUSINESS SUCCESS

Several factors contribute to the success of a business. While the specific factors can vary depending on the industry, market, and individual circumstances, here are some common elements that play a crucial role in business success:

VALUE PROPOSITION: Having a clear and compelling value proposition is essential. Businesses need to offer products or services that meet customer needs, solve problems, or provide unique benefits compared to competitors.

MARKET UNDERSTANDING: Understanding the target market, including customer preferences, demographics, and trends, is critical. This knowledge helps in tailoring products, marketing strategies, and customer experiences to maximize appeal and relevance.

EFFECTIVE LEADERSHIP: Strong leadership is vital for setting a clear vision, making strategic decisions, and inspiring and motivating employees. Effective leaders provide guidance, foster a positive organizational culture, and drive the business toward its goals.

CUSTOMER FOCUS: Placing customers at the center of business decisions and consistently delivering exceptional customer experiences is crucial. This includes providing excellent customer service, actively seeking feedback, and continuously adapting to meet evolving customer expectations.

QUALITY PRODUCTS OR SERVICES: Offering high-quality products or services that meet or exceed customer expectations is fundamental to success. Quality builds customer trust and loyalty, leading to repeat business and positive word-of-mouth recommendations.

OPERATIONAL EFFICIENCY: Efficient and streamlined operations help businesses minimize costs, maximize productivity, and deliver products or services in a timely manner. This includes optimizing processes, leveraging technology, and continually seeking ways to improve efficiency.

FINANCIAL MANAGEMENT: Effective financial management is vital for business success. This involves proper budgeting, cash flow management, financial forecasting, and maintaining profitability. Sound financial decisions and prudent resource allocation contribute to long-term sustainability.

INNOVATION AND ADAPTABILITY: Businesses need to embrace innovation, foster a culture of creativity, and adapt to changing market dynamics. This includes staying updated on industry trends, embracing new technologies, and being agile in response to market shifts.

MARKETING AND BRANDING: Developing a strong brand identity, implementing effective marketing strategies, and engaging in targeted promotional activities are crucial for attracting and retaining customers. Effective marketing helps businesses differentiate themselves and communicate their value to the target audience.

TALENT ACQUISITION AND DEVELOPMENT: Hiring and retaining skilled employees who align with the business's goals and values is essential. Investing in employee training, development, and creating a positive work environment fosters employee satisfaction, productivity, and loyalty.

PARTNERSHIPS AND COLLABORATION: Building strategic partnerships and collaborations can provide access to new markets, resources, expertise, and synergies. Collaborating with complementary businesses or industry stakeholders can enhance competitiveness and open up new opportunities.

It's important to note that these factors are interconnected, and the success of a business relies on a well-rounded approach that addresses multiple aspects simultaneously.

BUILDING A SOLID BUSINESS FOUNDATION

Several key factors contribute to the success of a business. While the specific elements can vary depending on the industry, market, and individual circumstances, a combination of various factors helps create a solid foundation for business success. Let's explore some of these factors in more detail:

VISION AND STRATEGY: A clear vision and a well-defined strategy are fundamental to business success. A compelling vision provides direction and purpose, while a robust strategy outlines the path to achieve the desired goals. It involves defining target markets, identifying competitive advantages, and establishing a roadmap for growth and development.

MARKET UNDERSTANDING: In-depth knowledge of the target market is crucial. Businesses must understand customer preferences, needs, and behaviors. Market research and analysis help identify trends, assess competition, and uncover opportunities. By understanding the market, businesses can tailor their products, services, and marketing strategies to meet customer demands effectively.

CUSTOMER FOCUS: Placing customers at the heart of the business is essential. Businesses need to understand and anticipate customer needs, provide exceptional experiences, and build strong relationships. By delivering value and exceeding expectations, businesses can foster customer loyalty, drive repeat business, and benefit from positive word-of-mouth referrals.

QUALITY PRODUCTS OR SERVICES: Offering high-quality products or services is a cornerstone of business success. Quality builds trust, enhances reputation, and differentiates a business from its competitors. Consistently delivering products or services that meet or exceed customer expectations is vital for long-term success and customer satisfaction.

EFFECTIVE LEADERSHIP: Strong leadership is critical for guiding a business toward success. Effective leaders inspire, motivate, and empower employees. They set a positive example, establish a supportive culture, and make strategic decisions that align with the business's goals. Leadership also involves fostering innovation, managing change, and promoting a strong work ethic.

OPERATIONAL EXCELLENCE: Efficient and streamlined operations are key to optimizing resources, reducing costs, and maximizing productivity. Businesses need to continuously improve processes, eliminate inefficiencies, and leverage technology to enhance operational effectiveness. By focusing on operational excellence, businesses can deliver products or services in a timely manner, improve customer satisfaction, and gain a competitive edge.

FINANCIAL MANAGEMENT: Sound financial management is crucial for business success. It involves prudent budgeting, cash flow management, financial forecasting, and profitability analysis. Businesses must effectively allocate resources, monitor financial performance, and make informed financial decisions. By maintaining healthy financials, businesses can ensure stability, fuel growth, and withstand economic fluctuations.

INNOVATION AND ADAPTABILITY: In today's rapidly evolving business landscape, innovation and adaptability are essential. Businesses need to embrace change, stay updated on industry trends, and proactively seek opportunities for improvement and growth. By fostering a culture of innovation, encouraging creativity, and being open to new ideas, businesses can stay ahead of the curve and remain competitive.

MARKETING AND BRANDING: Effective marketing and branding strategies are vital for attracting customers and building brand equity. Businesses need to develop a strong brand identity, create compelling messaging, and implement targeted marketing campaigns to reach their target audience. By effectively communicating their value proposition, businesses can enhance brand recognition, generate leads, and drive customer acquisition.

TALENT ACQUISITION AND DEVELOPMENT: Skilled and motivated employees are invaluable assets to a business. Hiring and retaining top talent that aligns with the business's values and goals is essential. Moreover, investing in employee training and development programs are key.

OWNING MORE THAN ONE BUSINESS

Owning multiple business organizations can indeed be a key factor in leveraging your time and achieving success. Here are a few reasons why:

DIVERSIFICATION: By owning multiple businesses across different industries or sectors, you can spread your risk. If one business faces challenges or market fluctuations, the others can provide a buffer and help maintain your overall financial stability.

ECONOMIES OF SCALE: Owning multiple businesses can allow you to benefit from economies of scale. You can consolidate resources such as purchasing, marketing, and administrative functions, which can reduce costs and increase efficiency. Shared resources and expertise can also enhance productivity and profitability across your businesses.

SYNERGIES: When businesses complement each other or have interdependencies, owning multiple organizations can create synergistic effects. For example, you can cross-promote products or services, share customer databases, or create joint ventures between your businesses. Such synergies can lead to increased revenue and market opportunities.

LEVERAGING EXPERTISE: As a business owner with multiple organizations, you can leverage your knowledge, skills, and experience across different industries. This can help you identify and capitalize on emerging trends, implement best practices, and transfer successful strategies from one business to another. By leveraging your expertise, you can accelerate growth and overcome challenges more effectively.

TIME MANAGEMENT: Owning multiple businesses allows you to delegate responsibilities and manage your time more efficiently. By having competent management teams or partners in place, you can focus on strategic decision-making, business expansion, or pursuing new opportunities. This enables you to multiply your impact and achieve more significant results than if you were solely focused on one business.

THE PROCESS AND WHAT OWNING MULTIPLE BUSINESSES CAN LOOK LIKE: It's important to note that owning multiple businesses also comes with challenges. It requires effective management, clear communication, and the ability to balance competing priorities. It's crucial to ensure each business receives adequate attention and resources to thrive. Additionally, regulatory and legal considerations may vary depending on the jurisdictions in which your businesses operate.

Overall, owning multiple business organizations can be a successful strategy for leveraging your time and achieving greater success, provided you have the necessary resources, expertise, and management capabilities to effectively oversee and grow each business.

THE IMPORTANCE OF FINANCIAL LITERACY AND HOW TO CREATE A STABLE AND HEALTHY BUSINESS WHILE INCORPORATING THE PROFIT FIRST METHOD.

IMPORTANCE OF FINANCIAL LITERACY:

a. DECISION-MAKING: Financial literacy equips business owners with the knowledge and skills to make informed decisions. It helps them understand financial statements, analyze financial data, and evaluate the financial implications of various choices. This enables them to make sound judgments about pricing strategies, investment opportunities, and resource allocation.

b. **FINANCIAL MANAGEMENT:** Effective financial management is fundamental to the success of any business. Financial literacy allows entrepreneurs to develop and implement strategies to manage cash flow, control expenses, and optimize profitability. It helps them understand key financial metrics, such as gross profit margin, net profit margin, and return on investment.

c. **RISK MANAGEMENT:** Financial literacy assists businesses in identifying and managing financial risks. By understanding concepts like diversification, insurance, and contingency planning, entrepreneurs can make informed decisions to mitigate risks and protect their businesses from financial setbacks.

d. **GROWTH AND EXPANSION:** Financial literacy plays a vital role in facilitating growth and expansion. It helps entrepreneurs understand the financial requirements and implications of scaling their operations. By analyzing financial data, projecting future cash flows, and assessing investment opportunities, business owners can make informed decisions to fuel growth while managing financial risks.

CREATING A STABLE AND HEALTHY BUSINESS WITH THE PROFIT FIRST METHOD:

The Profit First method is a financial management approach that involves dividing income into various accounts based on predetermined percentages, aiming to ensure sustainable profitability for a business. I personally use this method in my business, and I've found that regular review of allocations is crucial to ensure that the percentages are effective. As my business grew, these percentages needed frequent adjustments. Whenever I faced a shortfall, I adjusted the percentages to manage my finances effectively. Initially, it seemed complex, but with consistent practice, it became routine.

THE PROFIT FIRST METHOD TYPICALLY CONSISTS OF 5 FOUNDATIONAL BANK ACCOUNTS, WHICH ARE:

a. INCOME: This account is where all the income your business generates is deposited.

b. PROFIT: A percentage of the income is allocated to this account, which is intended for the business owner's profit distributions.

c. OWNER'S COMPENSATION: This account is designated to hold funds for the owner's salary or compensation.

d. TAX: A portion of the income is allocated to this account to ensure that funds are available to cover tax obligations.

e. OPERATING EXPENSES: This account holds the money needed to cover the day-to-day operating expenses of the business.

These accounts are the core of the Profit First method and are used to manage and allocate the business's income effectively.

In my experience, I transfer funds every two weeks on Tuesdays, as this is when all funds clear in my accounts. However, I understand that this schedule may not work for everyone. My advice for anyone interested in adopting this method is to seek the help of a CPA or bookkeeper who is knowledgeable about Profit First. Their expertise can help navigate the implementation process effectively.

You will also need some type of accounting system, such as QuickBooks, FreshBooks, Xero, or one of the many others available, to find the one that best suits your needs. Personally, I use QuickBooks and have found it easy to learn and use, especially with its helpful reports. It has aided me in understanding the percentages of each area of my business, which I then use to categorize and determine my percentages. For instance, the operations category includes expenses related to managing my business, such as rent, payroll, utilities, advertising, vehicle expenses, and more.

The percentages below are the percentages that I use in my business.

Please understand that financial percentages can vary for each business based on their unique needs and circumstances. It is important to know that these percentages can change as your business grows and evolves. I recommend seeking financial advice, especially using the profit first method to determine the right percentages for your business based on your specific requirements.

The profit first method advocated by Mike Michalowicz emphasizes setting aside profit first, and then allocating the remaining funds to expense. By following this approach, you can prioritize profitability and sustainable growth in your business. To establish the ideal percentages for your business according to the profit first method, it's advisable to consult with a financial advisor or accountant that may analyze your business, financial situation, cash flow and objectives to create a tailored financial plan that supports your business goals and ensures financial stability managing your finances effectively is crucial for the success of your business and seeking professional advice, can help you make informed decisions and achieve long-term financial success.

HERE'S THE BREAKDOWN OF THE ALLOCATION PERCENTAGES AND THE FORMULA USED FOR A TOTAL OF 100%:

- OPERATING EXPENSES ACCOUNT: 60% (including rent and payroll)
- OWNERS PAY ACCOUNT: 15%
- TAX ACCOUNT: 15%
- PROFIT ACCOUNT: 10%

WITH THESE PERCENTAGES, I DISTRIBUTE MY INCOME AS FOLLOWS:

- Revenue Account (100% of income goes here)
- Operating Expense Account (60% of income)
- Owners Pay Account (15% of income)
- Tax Account (15% of income)
- Profit Account (10% of income)

Every two weeks, I transfer the allocated percentages from the Revenue Account to the other four accounts, following the specified formula.

FOR EXAMPLE, IF MY REVENUE ACCOUNT RECEIVES $10,000, I DISTRIBUTE IT AS FOLLOWS:

- OPERATING EXPENSE ACCOUNT: $6,000 (60% of $10,000)
- OWNERS PAY ACCOUNT: $1,500 (15% of $10,000)
- TAX ACCOUNT: $1,500 (15% of $10,000)
- PROFIT ACCOUNT: $1,000 (10% of $10,000)

Adopting this method may require setting up automatic transfers and adjusting financial processes, but after using it, I've seen the benefits, including improved financial visibility and sustainable business growth.

In summary, financial literacy is crucial for businesses to make informed decisions, effectively manage their finances, and achieve long-term stability and growth.

By incorporating the Profit First method into your financial management practices, you can prioritize profit and cash flow, which are vital for the health of your business. Remember to assess your current financial situation, set realistic profit targets, allocate funds to different accounts based on percentages, regularly analyze and adjust your allocations, focus on expense management, and seek professional guidance when needed.

Additionally, it's important to continue learning and improving your financial literacy to stay informed and make better financial decisions for your business. Keep in mind that allocations percentages will be different for every business. Always remember to consult with your accountant or tax professional. Their expertise can provide valuable insights and guidance tailored to your specific financial situation and business needs.

(Business owners can benefit from having a diverse team with a range of expertise.)

HERE ARE THREE KEY ROLES THAT BUSINESS OWNERS SHOULD CONSIDER ADDING TO THEIR TEAM:

a. FINANCIAL ADVISOR/ACCOUNTANT: A financial advisor or accountant can provide crucial guidance on financial matters, including budgeting, tax planning, financial forecasting, and risk management. They can help the business owner make informed decisions about investments, funding, and financial strategies, ensuring the financial health and compliance of the business.

b. ATTORNEY: An attorney can provide legal counsel and representation, helping the business owner navigate complex legal issues such as contracts, business structure, intellectual property, compliance, and any potential disputes or litigation. They can also assist in risk management and ensure the business operates within the boundaries of the law.

c. MARKETING SPECIALIST: A marketing specialist can help the business owner create and execute effective marketing strategies to promote the business, attract customers, and increase sales. They can assist with market research, branding, advertising, social media management, and digital marketing to help the business reach its target audience and grow its customer base.

These professionals can provide specialized expertise and support, enabling the business owner to focus on the core aspects of running and growing the business.

By combining financial literacy with the Profit First method, you can create a solid foundation for your business and pave the way for sustainable profitability and success.

IN CONCLUSION

Starting and running a successful business is a challenging endeavor that demands careful attention to numerous interconnected factors. While every business is unique, certain fundamental principles can guide entrepreneurs toward success. This book explores the ten pillars that encapsulate these principles, covering areas such as strategic planning, market research, leadership, financial management, marketing, operations, human resources, customer relationship management, and continuous learning. By understanding and implementing these pillars, entrepreneurs can establish a solid foundation for their businesses and enhance their chances of long-term success.

Profit-oriented businesses are driven by the primary goal of achieving financial success while delivering exceptional service. The key to accomplishing this lies in the strategies we implement to organize and run our businesses effectively. When considering all aspects of our operations, including generating innovative ideas, utilizing the right tools, assembling a competent team, building a strong network, staying motivated, and ensuring customer satisfaction, we can set ourselves up for success. Business organization plays a pivotal role in this process, as a lack of it can lead to failure. I can personally attest to the importance of proper organization, as I once struggled with disorganization due to juggling multiple responsibilities simultaneously. This led to a loss of personal freedom and flexibility, a decline in income, and even negatively impacted my health. It was through this experience that I realized the need for change in order to salvage both my business and personal well-being.

For a long time, I was concerned about the challenges we as a community were facing for our young children due to the lack of quality educational programs. In the current situation where a significant number of households rely on both parents' income for contributions and provisions for household and family needs. Families are in a dilemma on what steps they should take to provide for their families while taking care of their young children and household needs.

At this time there are four key options for parents:

▶ Stay at home and take care of their young children.

▶ Pay for childcare.

▶ Use family and friends.

▶ Apply for state or federal-sponsored child care aid.

Opening and operating a high-quality educational program in my community became a pressing need. The lack of quality care and education was taking its toll on both myself and numerous families in the area. The idea of establishing a childcare program had been on my mind for years, as I wanted to make a difference by offering exceptional care and education. I was also determined to challenge the existing standards and stereotypes associated with childcare programs across the nation.

As a former educator, I understood the significance of education, particularly during the crucial developmental stages from infancy to five years old. As a parent of two young children, I recognized quality education was not a luxury but a necessity for my family. This drove my determination to ensure that my program would not be a mere babysitting service but a place that provided a safe, healthy, nurturing, and high-quality educational environment.

By opening and operating this program, I aimed to make a positive impact on the lives of children and families in our community. I wanted to create a space where children could thrive academically, socially, and emotionally, setting a new standard for childcare programs. Through my experience and dedication, I hoped to contribute to the growth and development of young minds, providing the foundation for their future success.

In 2016, I established my first program with the goal of creating a successful business and providing career opportunities for the community. I was thrilled when the program reached full capacity within its first year. To ensure quality education and support, I made sure all employees were certified and received ongoing training.

However, as the business boomed, I realized that managing it efficiently became a challenge. The program consistently had a waitlist of children, but the biggest obstacle was finding and retaining qualified staff. The COVID-19 pandemic further exposed the disorganization within my company. It was a wake-up call for me to reassess the overall performance and success of the business.

During the pandemic, many parents became concerned about the safety of their children, leading to a significant drop in enrollment. This sudden shift resulted in only 10% of the center's capacity being utilized. The staff members were understandably frightened, and some decided to leave due to the uncertainty surrounding the situation. However, a few dedicated staff members remained, despite their fears and the uncertainty.

It became evident that our emergency plans and parent handbooks were outdated and needed a thorough revision. Additionally, I realized that we lacked proper systems to handle crises or emergencies. It was clear that we were running the company more like a small, family-owned business rather than a professional corporation.

In response to these challenges, I took immediate action. The safety and well-being of the children became my top priority. I implemented strict health and safety protocols based on the guidelines provided by health authorities. This included enhanced cleaning procedures, social distancing measures, and mandatory mask-wearing for staff and older children.

Addressing the staffing issues, I focused on creating a supportive and positive work environment. I communicated transparently with the staff, assuring them of the measures being taken to ensure their safety and well-being. To boost their confidence and skills, I provided additional training opportunities.

Recognizing the need for better organization and preparedness, I worked on developing comprehensive emergency plans and updated the parent handbooks to include clear instructions and protocols for various scenarios. Regular drills and training sessions were established to familiarize the staff with these protocols and enable them to respond effectively during emergencies.

To transform the business into a more professional entity, I implemented systems and processes to enhance efficiency. This included adopting an electronic record-keeping system, automating administrative tasks, and utilizing software solutions for scheduling, communication, and enrollment management. These changes aimed to improve communication with parents, streamline operations, and reduce administrative burdens.

I also focused on building strong relationships with parents and the community. I increased communication channels, providing regular updates and addressing concerns promptly. Seeking feedback from parents, I implemented their suggestions whenever possible. By fostering a sense of community and involving parents in decision-making, I aimed to rebuild trust and confidence in our services.

The experience during the pandemic taught me valuable lessons about adaptability, preparedness, and continuous improvement. By addressing the weaknesses exposed, I transformed my business into a more resilient and professional organization. I am now better equipped to handle future challenges and position my school for long-term success.

The resignation of some of the employees created a void. Amongst the challenges I was facing, I realized that many staff members resigned for reasons that they were unwilling to disclose. I later discovered that the program disorganization in the company was of concern to them and one of the reasons for resigning.

The demand for more staff was inevitable as the number of parents seeking our services increased. The high demand for labor forced me to take part in the care and educational process. Initially, I could visit the center a few times a day to see the progress and address issues that might have come up that day. I could then leave them to continue with the care, engagement and education of the children. After the resignation of several staff members, it was a must to be present all the time to assist the remaining employees. For that reason, I lost my freedom and flexibility.

More importantly, the disorganization reduced my profit margins from the program. I was consistently working in the classrooms and not in the office. At that time, tuition was not being collected due to not having the proper systems in place causing reduced income. The program was operating with fewer staff, so it was not easy to meet the needs of all the children and families. I had to take weeks and months to train new staff due to not having a training system in place to properly train current and new employees.

I needed to find a solution that could sustain the program, considering the consequences of the disorganization on the overall business performance. It was necessary to focus on processes that could support employee retention and win customer trust and loyalty. I began to invest in myself through professional development trainings, reading motivational books, attending webinars and conferences, and collaborating with other business leaders.

One has to plan well and include strategies for future expectations and uncertainties.

My program's performance improved after considering the advice and the skills taught during all the training sessions I attended. I then began to incorporate all the lessons learned into practice in my personal life and my business. I spent long days and sleepless nights because I was determined to stop running my company as a mom and pop and wanted it to be a successful company with proper systems in place. One of the steps I took was introducing an excellent binder system to the program to ensure that files and data were stored well in a specific order. The disorganization made it challenging to locate the customer's files and company documents, which presented the business's weakness and disorganization. It was important to introduce a good record-keeping system to serve clients and staff effectively.

Also, I developed a standard operating procedure (SOP) that could guide the staff in day-to-day operations and organizational activities to encourage employee retention. The SOP captured all the processes that would take place in the course of the day as employees attended to the children. It specified the roles and duties for every employee in the business. In addition, I introduced online and in-person staff training programs. It was essential to train the staff on the skills and knowledge that could improve services. The skills would enhance customer satisfaction. I encouraged my staff to focus on the program's vision. More importantly, I put in place measures to reduce burnout. I replaced those who had resigned. I also added a policy that calls for the recruitment of an additional workforce if the number of children increases beyond a specified margin. I also had to put a digital payment system in place, especially during the current coronavirus pandemic. The payment system offered instant transactions and an online payment system where no interaction was needed. This eased payments and protected both the parents and the staff. We also added a parent engagement app so that the parents could see the activities of their children on a day to day basis which was instant and immediately accessible to their mobile devices. This created trust, security, and much more. Implementing these made the program well-organized and successful.

Running a successful childcare business requires a deep understanding of operations combined with extreme organization. Challenges can arise that limit business operations, so it's essential to proactively address them. Lack of organization can lead to negative consequences such as reduced income, limited freedom and flexibility, which can ultimately result in business failure.

To regain control of my time and achieve success, I discovered three organizational hacks that significantly helped me.

1. PRIORITIZING: I learned to identify and focus on the most critical tasks. By prioritizing effectively, I could allocate my time and resources more efficiently, ensuring that I addressed important issues and achieved essential goals for the business.

2. DELEGATING: I realized that I couldn't do everything myself, so I started delegating tasks to capable team members. Delegating not only lightened my workload but also

empowered my staff, allowing them to contribute their skills and expertise to the business's success.

3. PLANNING: I implemented effective planning strategies to anticipate challenges and seize opportunities. By setting clear goals, creating action plans, and establishing deadlines, I could stay on track and make progress toward achieving my objectives. Planning also enabled me to adapt to changing circumstances and make informed decisions.

Implementing these organizational hacks brought back my time and freedom, and my business started to grow and thrive. I attribute this success to the changes I made and the knowledge I acquired. As a business owner, I highly recommend continuous learning, attending conferences, and taking actionable steps. Embracing change may be challenging, but the rewards are worth it. Seeing the results of my hard work and witnessing my business succeed has been incredibly fulfilling.

Bold steps and unflagging determination are key to building a successful business. Though each business faces its own unique challenges and obstacles, *The Ten Pillars of Owning and Operating a Successful Business* will help you in any product or business type. The journey requires constant effort and unprecedented risk. But I assure you, it's worth it!

Ready to take your business to the next level?

Finally, after solving all the necessary changes, staying organized, prioritizing tasks, delegating responsibilities, and effective planning are crucial for running a successful childcare business. By implementing these strategies and continually learning and adapting, I overcame challenges, drove growth, and achieved long-term success.

I hope I was able to provide you with some immediate actionable items to get you started on your journey and that my experience was a lesson to guide you and your business to success.

INTERVIEWS

MAYEISHA PARKER
MFAStudios
Owner / Artistic Director

Q 1. What made you go into entrepreneurship?

As an aspiring entrepreneur, I decided to venture into entrepreneurship because of my deep passion for a particular field or industry. I wanted to return to doing something I loved and put so much of myself into. The idea of creating something meaningful and making a positive impact was a strong driving force for me.

Q 2. What is some advice that you recommend people do immediately?

If I had to give immediate advice to anyone looking to start their entrepreneurial journey, it would be to just do it. Waiting for the perfect moment or having everything figured out will only delay progress. Start taking action, even if it's starting small, and begin working towards your goals. Additionally, it's important to understand your target audience and their needs. Take the time to identify the market you want to serve and what specific problem or need you can fulfill for them.

Q 3. What are the worst things and best things that have happened to you as a business owner?

As for the best and worst things that can happen to a business owner, I have experienced both. One of the worst things I have faced is poor cash flow. Underestimating costs and not adequately preparing for slow times can lead to financial challenges and make it difficult to cover expenses or invest in growth opportunities. It's crucial to manage cash flow effectively and have contingency plans in place.

On the flip side, one of the best things about being a business owner is the sense of independence and control. Having the freedom to make your own decisions, set your own direction, and be your own boss can be incredibly rewarding. Additionally, the potential for financial success and wealth creation is another positive aspect that attracts many entrepreneurs. Building a successful business that generates profits and provides financial security is a significant achievement.

Overall, entrepreneurship is a journey that comes with its ups and downs, but pursuing something you are passionate about and taking calculated risks can lead to fulfilling and rewarding experiences.

KISHANI M. WOLDBERHAN
KIDS Early Learning Centers
Founder/CEO

EMAIL: Kidslearningcenters@gmail.com
TEL : (323) 627 6191

Q1. What made you go into Entrepreneurship ?

The reason I became an entrepreneur is because of many factors. The passion and purpose I had of providing a high quality learning environment to children around the world for one thing. It was also the independence in been my own boss, financial freedom, flexibility with work life balance, professional growth, and creating a lasting legacy.

Q2. What is some advice you recommend people do immediately?

Know your why and what your goals are, then work towards them with a plan.

Q3. What is the worst thing and best thing that has happened to you as a business owner?

The worst thing that has happened to me is that life is not easy. The journey to becoming a business owner has many ups and downs. Every time you rise up, people will pull you down. You need to know who your associates really are because everyone is not your friend and not everyone has your best interest at heart.

ROBIN HARRIS
Founder & CEO
Future Leaders Learning Academy

Q 1. What made you go into entrepreneurship?

I've always had a business mindset. As a child, I would make a price list and have relatives pay me for services such as yardwork, babysitting, and other tasks outside of my chores. It's always been near and dear to my heart. It's WHO I AM.

Q 2. What is some advice that you recommend people do immediately?

I recommend people find their groups and accountability partners, research daily and continue ongoing training. The business world changes daily. We must position ourselves to change and grow with it. There is no such thing as "knowing it all." Every day as an entrepreneur, I learn something new to take my business to the next level.

Also, get organized and truly hold yourself accountable. Make a list of duties and see them through. Plans without action are simply beautiful notes on paper. We must organize our thoughts and make things happen. Set realistic goals and timelines for yourself. Check them off and move to the next goal.

Q 3. What are the worst things and best things that have happened to you as a business owner?

The worst thing that ever happened to me as a business owner was surviving during COVID. It wasn't a pleasant experience at all. I remember tutoring my older students via ZOOM. Seeing them online crying and pleading to come to school broke my heart. There was literally nothing that I could do but PRAY! My school is home to so many students and it was so hard watching them experience the pandemic.

The best thing I ever experienced as a business owner is continuous... it's watching students learn objectives two to three levels above their own. Even outside of our campus, they practice higher level skills. One parent told me that her four-year-old gave her the amount of tax for her bill while at the store. Listening to parents pour their gratitude about their child's education makes my heart smile.

FINAL THOUGHTS

As I bring this book to a close, I want to express my deepest appreciation for the privilege of accompanying you on this transformative journey. Throughout these pages, my goal has been to provide you with valuable insights and practical tools to navigate the challenges that arise during the development and growth of your business. Entrepreneurship is a path riddled with obstacles, but it is also brimming with opportunities for personal and professional growth.

We all face struggles and setbacks along the way. It's an inherent part of the entrepreneurial journey. But what separates successful entrepreneurs from the rest is their ability to rise above those challenges, to persevere in the face of adversity, and to emerge stronger and wiser on the other side. It is in those moments of difficulty that we discover our true strength and resilience.

By sharing my own story, I hope to have shown you that success is not handed to us on a silver platter. It is earned through hard work, determination, and a relentless pursuit of our dreams. The journey may be arduous, but the rewards are immeasurable. The setbacks, the failures, and the doubts you encounter are not indicators of your inadequacy, but rather opportunities for growth and self-discovery.

Within the pages of this book, you have found a collection of tools, strategies, and insights that can serve as your guiding compass as you navigate the unpredictable waters of entrepreneurship. But remember, these tools are only as effective as your willingness to embrace them and put them into action. It is through action that dreams are transformed into reality.

I want to encourage you to dream bigger and better. Never settle for mediocrity or complacency. Continuously challenge yourself to push beyond your comfort zone, to explore uncharted territories, and to reach for new heights. Your potential is limitless, and the only thing that can hold you back is your own self-imposed limitations.

As you embark on this entrepreneurial journey, surround yourself with a supportive network of mentors, peers, and like-minded individuals who can inspire and uplift you during both the triumphs and the trials. Collaboration and community are essential components of success. Seek out opportunities for learning and growth, whether through industry conferences, workshops, or online resources. Stay curious, be open to new ideas, and never stop expanding your knowledge and skill set.

Remember that success is not solely measured by financial gain or external achievements. True success encompasses a sense of fulfillment, a genuine passion for what you do, and a positive impact on the lives of others. As you build your business, remain true to your values, and let them guide your decisions and actions. Embrace ethical and sustainable practices that uphold the well-being of both people and the planet.

Lastly, I want to express my sincere belief in your abilities and potential. You have embarked on a remarkable journey by choosing entrepreneurship, and I have no doubt that your dedication, perseverance, and unwavering spirit will lead you to great heights. Embrace the challenges as opportunities for growth and transformation. Trust in yourself and your unique talents. And never lose sight of the dreams and aspirations that ignited your entrepreneurial flame.

Thank you for allowing me to be a part of your journey. May this book serve as a source of inspiration, guidance, and empowerment as you navigate the ever-evolving landscape of entrepreneurship. Dream big, aim high, and create a future that surpasses your wildest imagination. The world is waiting for your brilliance. Now go out there and make your mark.

ACKNOWLEDGMENTS

I would like to express my deepest gratitude and appreciation to my other half, children, family, and friends. Your unwavering support has been the bedrock of my journey.

To all my readers who have joined me on this journey, I am truly thankful for your presence and support.

I would also like to extend my heartfelt thanks to Lil Barcaski, my dedicated book editor/publisher and the team at GWN Publishing Company. Your expertise and commitment have been instrumental in bringing this book to fruition. This would not have been possible without all of you, and I am deeply grateful for your contributions.

To the readers who have embraced *The Ten Pillars of Owning and Operating a Successful Business*, I am sincerely thankful. It is my hope that this book impacts your life in a meaningful way, just as it has transformed mine. This book stands as a testament to the collective support and inspiration that have shaped its creation. I am humbled and honored by the role each of you has played in bringing this work to life. Thank you from the very depths of my heart. This book would not have been possible without you all.

ABOUT THE AUTHOR

Samantha Zayas is a successful entrepreneur who has overcome significant hurdles in her life to emerge as a prominent figure in the business world. Her personal journey has been characterized by resilience and an unwavering determination to succeed.

Drawing from the challenges she has faced, Zayas has been motivated to pursue a career as a successful businesswoman and entrepreneur. Her experiences have instilled in her a deep commitment to motivating others to pursue their dreams and to strive for generational wealth for themselves and their families.

Through her actions and achievements, Zayas serves as a living example of the transformative power of perseverance and dedication. Zayas' story embodies the belief that dreams can indeed become reality, and her journey stands as an inspiration to all those who aspire to carve their own path to success. Her unwavering spirit and dedication to empowering others serves as a testament to the potential for individuals to turn their aspirations into tangible achievements.

www.ingramcontent.com/pod-product-compliance
Lightning Source LLC
Chambersburg PA
CBHW060310130626
46546CB00015B/914